THE BREAK UP JOURNAL

A Guide To Get Over Your Ex & Fall Back In Love With Yourself

BLAKE C. HOLLAWAY

DISCLAIMER: The information in this book is intended for educational and entertainment purposed only. It is sold with the understanding that neither the author nor the publisher is engaging in rendering accounting, legal, medical, psychological, therapeutic or other professional services. This book is not intended to serve as the basis for medical or psychological decisions. You should seek the services of a competent professional for expert assistance pertaining to your specific situations.

While the publisher and author have used their best efforts in preparing this book, they make no representations or warranties with respect to the accuracy or completeness of the contents of this book and specifically disclaim any implied warranties of merchantability or fitness for a particular purpose. No warranty may be created or extended by sales representatives or written sales materials. The advice and strategies contained herein may not be suitable for your situation. You should consult with a professional where appropriate. Neither the publisher nor the author shall be liable for any of your actions and specifically disclaim responsibility for any liability, loss, risk or any physical, psychological, emotional, financial, or commercial damages personal or otherwise, that incurred directly or indirectly from the use or application of any contents in this publication, including but not limited to special, incidental, consequential, personal, or other damages.

Book Cover by Blake C. Hollaway
Photo Credit: Robert La Mantia
The Break Up Journal: A Guide To Get Over Your Ex And Fall Back In Love With Yourself/ Blake C. Hollaway - 1st ed

ISBN: 979-8-9903840-0-2 (paperback)

This journal is dedicated to my brother and anyone else who was unable to get the help they needed and deserved, to my mom who taught me how to fight impossible battles, to my sisters and the hope for brighter generations, as well as to those who have felt lost, broken, unworthy, or unloved, and who have gazed upon the vast expanse of the starlit sky, longing or dreaming for something more.

Table of CONTENTS

Table of CONTENTS CONT'D

CHAPTER *One*

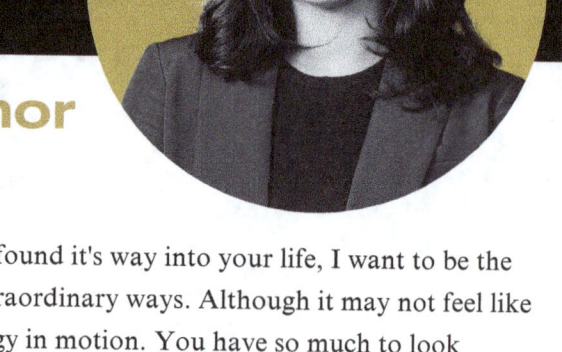

A Note From The Author

Hello Beautiful Soul,

If you are reading this right now and this journal has found it's way into your life, I want to be the first to tell you that your life is about to change in extraordinary ways. Although it may not feel like it right now, you have already set this wonderful energy in motion. You have so much to look forward to and these extraordinary changes are making their way into your life right now as you read this.

I won't pretend to know the circumstances that led you to this journal or the exact challenges you may be facing. However, I firmly believe that our paths crossing in this encounter is not merely coincidental. I want you to know that no matter where you are at on your journey, things can get better.

Although this book primarily focuses on breakups, I understand the profound sense of isolation that arises when your experiences alienate you from the rest of the world. It's a journey where pain and suffering become so familiar, they simultaneously feel like companions and part of your identity. I have felt the overwhelming paralysis that accompanies staring down at all the broken fragments and not knowing where to start, realizing that even if they could be reassembled, even with all the time in the world to try, the resulting entity would bear little resemblance to its former self. This is the profound and all-encompassing loss that comes with losing yourself.

Yet, I've also embarked on the arduous journey of piecing together each sliver and fragment, emerging from the chaos forever transformed. I know the freedom that comes from understanding and releasing your pain. I know the peace that initially feels unsafe when you first truly begin to heal and then introduces you to a way of being you didn't know existed. Through this process of destruction and reconstruction, I've come to understand how love has the power to fill the chasms between the broken pieces so completely the scars are barely noticeable even to you. To find the light in the dark, you must first open your eyes.

For many years, I have kept what I have always referred to as my Book of Sacred. This sacred book is a journal I keep that houses all my shadow work, my thoughts, affirmations, manifestations and more. For the first time, I am sharing some of these methods I have built for myself over a lifetime of inner work with you to help you on your journey of self discovery, healing and love. Welcome to my inner circle of guidance and I would like to formally introduce you to your very first and very own Book of Sacred: The Break Up Journal: A Guide To Get Over Your Ex & Fall Back In Love With Yourself

This guided journal is here to support you on your journey of healing from recent or not-so-recent breakups. While the term "breakup" often makes us think of romantic relationships, it's important to remember that separations can occur in various types of relationships and for a variety of reasons. Whether it was a mutual decision or initiated by one person, a breakup signifies that you, the other person, or both of you have chosen to part ways in some capacity from each other's lives.

This process, regardless of who initiated it, is a journey that can feel very isolating and painful. But I want you to know that you are not alone in this process nor are you now or have you ever been truly alone. With this sacred book I impart to you, it is my intention to help you heal, find closure, break negative cycles, re-align and reunite with the most important soulmate you will ever meet. **You.**

I am so happy you are here and so proud of the efforts you are putting into creating an abundant future for yourself. You are a powerful and amazing human being. You just may have forgotten that truth about yourself and need to get reacquainted with that part of yourself you buried beneath the surface. Remember, all the magic in this life begins with you. As always may your life be full of light, full of love, abundance and gratitude.

All My Love & Gratitude,

Blake Holloway

CHAPTER *Two*

Some Tips Before You Get Started...

Tip 1

Take This Journey At Your Own Pace

The path to healing is far from linear. There will be days when your progress takes the lead, and other days when your wounds, pain, or disappointments might have the upper hand. Emotions themselves can arrive like waves, rising and subsiding like the tide. As you journey through this process, remember to go at your own pace and avoid rushing it. Regardless of how you feel about the relationship or the other person involved, this process is **FOR YOU**. Your well-being is a priority, and honoring your own timing is an essential part of that and self care. It's time to give yourself the unconditional love, respect, energy and time that you give everyone else.

Tip 2

This Journey Is About You & For You

It can be easy in a relationship or while navigating a break up for our focus to shift to the other person - what they did right or what they did wrong. However, it's crucial to recognize that this journey and the healing process are all about you. This journal is specifically crafted to center on your healing, your responsibility, your accountability, your alignment, and your happiness. While certain parts of this journal might prompt you to reflect on the other person or the relationship, always keep in mind that the focus of this journey belongs to you. It's your personal path to growth and healing. This path may look different for everyone, and my hope is that you will discover the route that works best for you.

It's also important to emphasize that part of this journey involves taking accountability for what is yours to take responsibility for and then coming to terms with it. Equally important is the act of releasing what was not meant for you to carry. As you work through this journal, embrace the empowering process of discerning what belongs to your growth and what can be gently released with gratitude, allowing you to lighten your load.

Throughout this book, we will work to build a solid foundation in the areas of emotional, mental, physical and spiritual wellbeing. When you have a solid foundation to build upon, you can navigate life's challenges with greater resilience, clarity, and purpose, enabling you to pursue your goals and aspirations with confidence and fulfillment.

Tip 3

Take What Resonates & Leave What Doesn't

This journal blends spiritual insights and tools with practical advice. I did my best to tailor it to various situations, but each person's journey of healing and love is truly unique. The techniques used in this book may not work for every one and every situation. It also touches on many specific topics but does not cover them all. I urge you to be open-minded to change, new mindsets, new perspectives and new ways of feeling, thinking and being. Feel free to substitute words like Spirit, angels, the universe, etc. with whatever terms resonate with you. If some sections don't perfectly align with your personal experience, focus on what truly resonates and works best for you. My intention is to guide you in viewing things from different perspectives as part of this transformative process. Embrace what resonates, integrate it into your life, and let go of what doesn't work for you or serve you.

Tip 4

The Truth About Self Care

There is a common misconception about self-care. While it's often associated with luxurious bubble baths and indulgent treats, the essence of self-care goes beyond these surface-level experiences. Genuine self-care includes sitting with and acknowledging all your emotions, facing both the unattractive and beautiful truths of a situation, and addressing challenges directly without letting them overpower you. True self-care can sometimes be uncomfortable and draining. This is why it's vital to discern when it's necessary to engage in the hard work and when it's time to take a pause or infuse joy.

Your body can serve as a guide, indicating when you need to exert effort and when you need rest. However, it's equally important to recognize that your senses might mislead you during difficult or emotional times. Feeling fatigued might be a result of sadness or depression rather than physical tiredness. You might resist company when in fact, being around others could be the best medicine for you. Embrace the notion of gently pushing yourself while also attuning to your genuine needs. It's crucial to stay grounded amidst the chaos that life can sometimes bring and always listen to your intuition. Your intuition is safe guidance.

I encourage you to remain mindful that not all healing has to be painful. Even though it might frequently feel uncomfortable, it is not a requirement to produce results. I encourage you not to put emotional expectations on your healing journey and allow the emotions to appear without forcing specific outcomes. You will get better results.

Tip 5

Create Healthy Separation

When we encounter someone or go through an experience, the energy becomes a part of us. The extent of this integration depends on the impact that person or experience had on our lives, be it substantial or slight. Throughout this journey, I encourage you to entertain the notion that these experiences might be companions we carry with us. Emotions are intricate and rarely black and white, but what you do with them is what matters. You can hold love for someone while recognizing their unsuitability for you. You can choose to leave someone, knowing it's the right choice, and still grieve their absence. Instead of attempting to eradicate or suppress these emotions entirely, we will focus on crafting a healthy space for them to exist. This space will enable them to coexist in a balanced and productive manner without commandeering your life.

Much like arranging belongings in your home, we will work to designate a safe and healthy space for these experiences and emotions.Through this journal you can dedicate time to your healing and understanding of them. This allocation will allow you to make room for other facets of your life. As time goes by, these experiences or emotions may become less intense, tumultuous or even disappear entirely. However, while we're in the process of healing, it's important for you to embrace all your feelings and emotions without allowing yourself to drown in them. Accept how you feel without judgement or avoidance. This is a crucial part of the healing journey, and it's okay to acknowledge and experience every aspect of it at your own pace.

Tip 6

The Past Doesn't Have To Define You

I'd like to share something interesting with you. The members of my inner circle and those I have helped along my path, who are privy to the experiences I've journeyed through in my life, frequently comment that I appear vastly different from my past and what was likely to result from my past. My childhood was difficult and I had to choose to survive a lot of pain, loss, trauma, sexual abuse and addiction. They often inquire how I reached this point and what steps I took to recover from my history. The response is actually quite straightforward: I made a conscious decision that my past wouldn't dictate my future. By making this decision, I began to stop identifying with the things from my past that did not align with the future I wanted for myself. I simply decided and make shifts to my desired perspective. But deciding was not enough. I also became the version of myself that no longer was victimized by my past.

Please understand that I don't say this flippantly; I recognize firsthand how challenging it can be. But it's true – your past doesn't have to mean anything about your future and the same goes for your relationships. You possess the power to rewrite your story at any given moment. Know that things can and will improve. The first step is simply deciding it is so and making the shifts to becoming the version of you that you desire to be.

Tip 7

Your Attraction, Worth & Value Are Not Determined By The Ability Or Inability Someone Else Has To See or Or Recognize It

I want you to set aside what other people have told you, what society has told you, what the dark side of you that is full of doubt and fear has told you or what you think is possible for yourself. You are attractive. You are worthy. You are valuable. Why? Because you are. It truly is that simple. No one's inability to see that diminishes who you really are. Surround yourself with people who not only recognize and appreciate your inherent value and worth, but who also inherently understand it without the need for guidance or negotiation.

It is my hope that this journal aids you in regaining your power and embracing confidence. You are a powerful presence in this world. Your perspective is unparalleled, entirely your own. Among the billions, there's no replication of you. You stand alone, uniquely and wonderfully you. That light is a gift. Don't ever let anyone dim it, but most importantly, never allow yourself to dim it in order to be more understood or accepted by someone else. Anyone who requires that kind of sacrifice of you is not your person.

Tip 8

The Work Is Not What Makes You Worthy

The manifestation tools I provide in this book serve to align you with the right energy. They're intended to help you become a magnet for the energies you desire in your life. These tools are not here to make you worthy; your worthiness is inherent. The universe doesn't attach conditions or stipulations to its gifts or its love. Its energy isn't biased. Instead, it simply mirrors back what you contribute. That is how powerful you are. Which is why it is important to spend time aligning to the energies you want to manifest. Your value is a constant and it is unwavering. You are deserving of all the positivity, happiness and abundance the universe has to offer. All you have to do is claim it. You do this by being intentional with the power you had inside you all along.

Tip 9

Learn To Find Happiness & Fulfillment From Within

The energy behind making changes and pursuing your goals, because it supports you and aligns with your best interests, differs significantly from taking action solely to prove your worth. True success, in any scenario, is a mindset not a destination. It arises from the belief that you are already the person you aspire to be; your accomplishments merely amplify the essence of who you are. As long as you continue seeking validation and self-worth through your achievements or external validation, the more success you achieve, the more unfulfilled you'll become. The cycle is never ending and you will always be racing to the next best thing, unable to live in or find joy in the moment.

You may think this is inapplicable to relationships, but challenges around self-worth, happiness and self-awareness bleed into all areas of your life. Sometimes the answers you seek to the obstacles you are experiencing lie in the most unexpected places.

Tip 10

Don't Attach Your Happiness or Self Worth To The Outcome

When we aspire to lead extraordinary lives, we often desire the extraordinary. This pursuit can lead to an addiction to the intense oscillations between soaring highs and crushing lows, which can be alluring due to their unmistakable intensity. However, it's essential to consider embracing the possibility of living an extraordinary life that doesn't rely on such volatile energy. Fulfillment, happiness, joy and abundance can also be found in consistency, steadiness, and tranquility.

What I've noticed both in others and in my own journey is the tendency to link self-worth and happiness to perceived success and the achievement of desires. This mindset, where fulfillment is believed to be attainable only at the endpoint, often leads to impatience. Consequently, we may make decisions merely to tick off boxes or to present well on paper, without genuinely fulfilling ourselves. In this rush, we forget to savor the journey, lacking consciousness in the present moment and overlooking seemingly insignificant moments that, in hindsight, held great importance.

This cycle not only perpetuates a need for external validation but also nurtures a lack of fulfillment. As we evolve and our desires grow, this cycle continues indefinitely. With each new desire, the pursuit of happiness becomes a never-ending chase.

In relationships, this pattern manifests as negative cycles of karmic relationships. It's crucial to learn to maintain your happiness, self-esteem, and sense of worth independently from your relationship, partner, or status.

Tip 11

There Is No Justification That Excuses Abuse & Unconditional Love Is Not Limitless Tolerance

Abuse takes various forms, but its root intention remains consistent: it aims to induce fear, intimidate, manipulate, harm, assign blame, shame or degrade someone in order to establish control. Abuse is not love and has no intention to love.

Unconditional love does not mean you must put up with anything and everything. It means that love is given freely without expectation or conditions for the love to be given. Unconditional love is to accept and love someone for who they really are, but that does not mean to tolerate any and all behavior. Love can forgive, but it is not limitless tolerance. Love alone is not enough to sustain a relationship and not all forms of love are unconditional. Some people can only offer you the level or depth of love to which they understand at the time. Others cannot offer you any form of real love at all.

Ensuring your safety is of utmost importance. If you suspect or are certain that you were or are in an abusive relationship, or if you're concerned about the possibility of your abuser returning, I strongly encourage you to seek professional assistance. You can reach out to the National Domestic Violence Hotline at 800-799-7233 for help and support. Many cities also have local resources that can help.

Tip 12

It's Okay To Ask For & Seek Help

Navigating a breakup and the subsequent healing journey can often evoke feelings of isolation. Nonetheless, it's crucial to realize that you don't have to brave this journey in solitude. Your inner circle is readily available to extend their support during trying moments. If you discover the need for additional guidance, I strongly encourage you to consider seeking aid from professionals like therapists, medical providers, coaches, and individuals who are skilled in helping you navigate your route to healing and self-discovery. Be an advocate for your own wellbeing.

Please note that I am not a medical health provider, psychologist or therapist. This book does not serve as a substitute for proper medical or professional care. Nor does it diagnose any mental or physical ailment.

Tip 13

Closure & Forgiveness Are Things You Give Yourself

Regardless of the words exchanged between you and the person you may have wronged, or those who wronged you, healing won't be instantaneous. Words and apologies can't magically erase pain. Endless discussions won't necessarily provide the closure or healing you seek. Often, when someone causes us harm, they may not even fully grasp the extent or impact of their actions. And even if they do understand, acknowledgment alone often falls short in alleviating pain or disappointment.

Forgiveness and closure is a path towards personal liberation. It's not about discounting or dismissing the wrong committed. It's about releasing the burden that carrying resentment, anger, shame or guilt places on your own well-being. As you travel through this journal, my wish for you is to rediscover your personal power. I hope you uncover a pathway to your own closure and forgiveness – whether it's for yourself or for those who have wronged you. These profound acts of healing are not contingent upon external validations or explanations; they originate within you and hold the potential to lead you towards a place of peace and release. These are gifts you give yourself and do not have the same effect when given by someone else.

Tip 14

The Only Way Is Through. Do The Work Darling

Although I have done my best to offer valuable perspectives, tools, and information in this book, the most effective results will emerge when you genuinely desire to receive them. Healing becomes possible only when your heart is genuinely committed to the process, and the commitment stems from a sincere desire. Your freewill means that this work must be done by you and for you. No matter the help you receive, how gifted the individual providing the help, or how enticing the incentive, if your commitment to healing and to improvement is not authentic, your timeline will not shift consistently or dramatically enough for you to see long term results.

The only way to get rid of pain, suffering and other negative emotions is to feel them, accept them, address them and heal them. Avoidance or choosing numbness will not prevent you from the experience of the negative emotions. Unhealed emotions and energies we avoid not only prolong our experience of them, but they are contagious. They end up being infused into the lives of our friends and family in various ways, some obvious and others much more subtle. The good news is that negative energy can be transmuted into positive energy with a bit of work and can even be used in a productive manner. Do the work. The avoidance and the numbness will always cause more destruction and suffering than the emotion itself.

Tip 15

Be Honest With Yourself. Dishonesty Is A Disservice To Yourself & Others

To truly embody authentic energy, it is essential to confront our desires and emotions honestly. This becomes especially crucial in the face of painful or traumatic events, where our instinct is often to evade the associated emotions. The challenge lies in the fact that emotions, whether positive or negative, are interconnected; you can't turn off one without turning them all off.

This suppression doesn't just lead to stagnant and unbalanced energy, potentially manifesting in negative ways and even physical ailments; it also severs our connection to intuition and the divine feminine energy present in all of us. This divine feminine energy gives power to our emotional, nurturing, and creative aspects which are crucial elements for manifesting our desires. When we close ourselves off from this energy, the ability to materialize our desires can become challenging.

Bottling up emotions creates a buildup of energetic and emotional pressure. Eventually, this pressure seeks release, often in detrimental ways, and is more likely to explode at the slightest pressure. I often use the analogy of emotions being like bubbles in champagne. The carbonation exists regardless of the bottle, but the one that is shook causes pressure to build up, leading to an explosive release. But the bottle you open calmly and pour carefully, you control the carbonation's pressure, allowing for a smooth, controlled and intentional release.

It is a common misconception that avoiding the experience or acknowledgement of emotions is controlling them. Emotions are transitioning energies. They are meant to flow. They can be a great indication of what is and is not working in your life at the time. Instead of trying to control the emotion itself, learn to understand them. By understanding them you can choose to act with intention instead of reacting. Like the champaign bottle, it's about controlling the pressure not the bubbles or carbonation.

We can control emotional pressure by providing a safe space for our feelings. Acknowledging and working through emotions prevents them from hijacking our lives. Suppressing our emotions is a disservice to ourselves and others. By navigating our feelings consciously, we retain control over the pressure, ensuring a more balanced, harmonious and authentic existence.

Tip 16

There Is No Line Between Here & There

When we undergo change, we often envision how it will unfold and what the outcome will look like. We imagine a clear separation between our present situation and the new reality, anticipating a sudden shift once we cross that imagined line. Whether in relationships, our healing journey, or manifestation efforts, we tend to view progress as a linear journey, like moving along a train track from one point to another.

However, the reality is that change is a transition that is not always linear, and there's rarely a distinct boundary between the before and after. The journey isn't straightforward, and neither is the change it brings. Progress is often subtle, lacking the definitive line we expect. Sometimes, we've already crossed that line without realizing it, and other times, progress occurs quietly in the background, even when it feels like nothing is happening.

Many of the small, seemingly insignificant steps we take daily contribute to the long-term, sustainable progress that eventually leads to the significant shifts we recognize as breakthroughs. Be patient through the transitions.

Tip 17

It All Begins With You

In the game of chess, the highest accolade a player can obtain is the title of Grandmaster. Once bestowed, this title is held for a lifetime. While a select number of Grandmasters exist worldwide, they epitomize excellence. I share this insight to emphasize that everything you desire originates with you. Much like a chess Grandmaster, you hold the status of Grandmaster in your life and in the art of manifesting. You wield the power to determine which pieces enter the game, how they're positioned, and how you navigate challenges. Just as a Grandmaster shapes the outcome of a chess match, you mold the trajectory of your life.

Humans are reservoirs of immense power. Our gift of freewill isn't coincidental; it empowers us to create, transform, and influence energy. I share these truths because as you embark on this journey and engage with this book, I hope you rediscover how powerful you really are. I wish for you to embrace every facet, both the beautiful and the chaotic, that composes your singular soul. You possess power. You exude beauty. You are cherished. And it all commences with you, the Grandmaster of Manifestation.

Tip 18

Find Joy In Not Having All The Answers

When we go looking too hard for the answer or get lost in the little details, we miss the big picture.

When experiencing painful or uncomfortable experiences, we tend to try to predict everything that is coming in hopes to gain stability, clarity or control. We want all the answers and when we don't have them, we panic or hyper fixate. Any answers you seek will come exactly when you need them. Trust the process and trust yourself to gain clarity. But also learn to find the joy in not having all the answers. Sometimes the universe delivers beautiful surprises in the most unexpected of ways and we are gifted with better then we could ever imagine.

Tip 19

The Victim Always Loses

Authors decide what happens in a story, and the greatest main characters they write tend to be those that are called active characters. These are characters that make decisions in the narrative instead of just allowing things to happening to them. Be careful of the narrative you write for yourself and the narrative of your life you tell others. It becomes your reality, your expectations, your perception and the perception others have of you.

You are simultaneously the author and main character of your own life. The Universe is not conspiring against you. In fact, the universe is always working in your best interest. Sometimes things will happen that are not in your control. However, you can control how you react to any situation, what stories you choose to write about your experiences and how those experiences influence you. Be an active participant in your own life. Be the hero of your own story not the victim. The victim always loses.

Tip 20

You Will Find Happiness Again

No matter how you are feeling right now or how bleak things may seem, I want to remind you that you will find happiness again. Things can and will get better no matter how far away that may seem. But it's important to remember that happiness is part of the magic that you create from within. It is ultimately a choice. By deciding and choosing happiness, you start to become happy.

There is a healthy amount of grief that can come with a separation. It is important to remember during times such as these that your happiness is your own responsibility. Better days are around the corner so try to keep your head up. You will smile again. You will laugh again. You will love again. The opportunities will present in the right time. So choose happiness. Choose what lights you up and fills you with joy. Seize the opportunities to become happy no matter how seemingly small. Make space to allow those that add to your happiness to enter your life.

Tip 21

The Amount of Time You Grieve Does Not Measure How Deep You Loved

Sometimes we opt to linger in our grief rather than actively pursuing healing. This choice may stem from a misconception that the pain will allow us to feel closer to the person we've lost or the misconception that the intensity and duration of our sorrow is a direct reflection of the depth of our love for that individual. However, the truth is, the duration of your grieving process does not measure the depth of your emotions. Clinging to pain won't alter the past; instead, it hinders your progress toward the future.

The bitterness of emotional pain can be like a lemon. When fixated on it, it's as if you're biting directly into a lemon. The taste will be overwhelming and bitter. But by making space for other aspects of your life, it’s like squeezing a lemon into water. You can still taste the lemon, but the bitterness is more tolerable. Grant yourself the space to heal and welcome the potential for a brighter future. Honor your journey by allowing a reasonable amount of time for grief, and then allow a new way of being to blossom.

Tip 22

Shame Is Not A Productive Motivator Be Curious Not Judemental

It is crucial as you move through this journal that you work to observe without judgment. Shame can impede deep self-reflection and the awareness necessary for healing. Shame also perpetuates a cycles of unworthiness, making it an unsustainable and unproductive motivator. Be gentle with yourself and grant yourself compassion. Use your curiosity to your advantage by using it peel back the many layers of yourself. You will be naturally curious towards that which will help you on your journey. It's okay to recognize your strengths and be aware of any areas in need of improvement. Strengthen yourself through awareness and unconditional self-love, knowing that growth is achievable without shame or harsh judgment. Provide yourself with healthy support instead.

Tip 23

Your Future Is Not In Your Past

To truly heal and move on from the past, embracing acceptance and release is crucial. These steps are pivotal and cannot be overlooked or brushed aside. Neglecting either one or both hinders progress, as they are imperative for forward movement.

In reality, your past only maintains its presence through your memories. Beyond these recollections, it ceases to exist, becoming a chapter that has concluded. Its continuation is solely contingent upon your choice to revisit it through memories.

Certain therapies and treatments may prove less effective when the result causes you to incessantly relive the past. This serves little purpose, yields no growth and does not allow you to show up as the latest version of yourself. Repetitively dwelling on the same moments offers no new insights and only perpetuates the past's influence on the present. Your mind and your body do not know the difference between what is and what has been. There is no distinguishable difference between past or present energy. Your mind and body therefore respond to that energy as if it is really happening every time you relive it. Reliving your past will not heal you. The past cannot be altered.

Accept what has happened, carry any lessons forward with you, send love and light to that which you remember fondly, but release everything else. Do not continue to live in your past by reliving it over and over in your mind and in this healing work. Look back only with intention, gain insight, express gratitude, release and/or apply lessons. Leave all else behind where it belongs. Do not shrink yourself to fit into the places you have outgrown.

Tip 24

Defining A Healthy Relationship

A healthy relationship may vary for each individual in terms of its specific components. However, fundamentally, it prioritizes desire over necessity. Wanting someone in your life because they contribute to your happiness differs significantly from needing someone because your happiness is contingent on that person or their presence. A healthy relationship should enhance the positive qualities between partners and radiate an overall aura of positivity. Love, in its purest form, is not control, entrapment, dependency, unlimited tolerance, judgment, selfishness, neglect, obsession, possessiveness, conditional or any other negative attribute. Pure, unconditional love is and exhibits only positive energy.

Tip 25

You Are The Person You Have Always Been Waiting For

Humans are inherently powerful beings. We wield the remarkable ability to shape, alter, or dispel energy. I reiterate this point to underscore its significance. I want you to truly grasp the extent of your power. The universe operates by the law that similar energies attract one another. Therefore, the energy you emit into the universe will inevitably draw back an energy like it. With this reality in mind, a fundamental truth emerges: to invite more love into our lives – whether it's romantic, platonic, or familial – we must first nurture a deeper source of love within ourselves. For this reason, cultivating self-love is of utmost importance.

Every trait and characteristic you've sought in someone else has always existed within you. The person you've been anticipating is, in fact, you. Love is an innate part of you, flowing effortlessly through your life. You stand as your own closest friend, nurturing parent, harshest critic, and unwavering supporter. Embrace the empowering truth that you possess the qualities you seek and journey forward with the radiant confidence that you are your own greatest source of love and strength. It all begins with you. Are you ready?

CHAPTER *Three*

ANOINT THIS JOURNAL

I began calling my Books of Sacred by this name because I thought it was a fitting name. They hold sacred knowledge and therefore should be treated with love, care and respect. No one should read or touch your Books of Sacred without your permission. Keep them hidden and protected.

Everything is made up of energy. While this journal has been infused with my positive intentions to promote healing, self-awareness, love, and abundance, it's essential for you to infuse your personal intentions and energy into its pages.

Intention is powerful. It allows the energies to be more focused on what you want to align to and sets spiritual boundaries for the energy. Think of manifesting as placing your order at a restaurant. You don't go into a restaurant and tell the server you just want to eat dinner. You would be at risk of receiving anything and everything the restaurant had to offer, including the fish you don't like, the nuts you are allergic to or the delicious cheese you have had before that you know gives you gas. No. You tell the server exactly what you want and how you want it. The universe is the server. It wants to bring you everything you desire. Being too vague leaves things open to wide interpretation. Being too specific can prevent you from trying something better you never thought up because there was no room for suggestion.

Through anointing your Book of Sacred, AKA this journal, you're purifying its energy to work in harmony with your needs, embedding your intentions to harmonize with the appropriate energies, and providing energetic protection to its pages. I'll reveal some of the methods I use to anoint my own Books of Sacred, but there's no fixed right or wrong approach. Trust your intuition and feel free to adapt this practice to suit your preferences and requirements. The intensity of this practice can be as intricate or simple as you are intuitively drawn to.

Some of these things might strike you as unconventional or even silly, but ever since I started incorporating them into my own Books of Sacred several years ago, I've experienced more favorable outcomes compared to the times when I wasn't engaging in them. I have even had people stumble upon the journals and immediately dismiss them without knowing why.

Anointing your Book of Sacred constitutes a spiritual ritual that maintains your journals' "energetic purity" and establishes guidelines for how energies operate for you. If this concept feels unfamiliar, envision it as upholding spiritual hygiene to keep your energies balanced and clear.

ANOINTING PRACTICE

STEP 1: CREATE SPACE

Begin by finding a calm, quiet and safe space to begin your practice where you won't be disturbed or interrupted.

STEP 2: CLEANSE

Cleans the energy. You can do this a number of ways. You can burn incense or herbs, sprinkle salt or simply visualize the journal and your space being engulfed in an orb of white light.

STEP 3: LET THE BOOK GET FAMILIAR WITH YOUR ENERGY

You can do this in a number of ways. Hug the journal tightly, sleep with it next to you or under your pillow, carry it with you for a day or visualize your energy flowing from your hand to the pages.

STEP 4: PROTECT

I personally like to set intentions that set spiritual and energetic boundaries around my Books of Sacred. I do this by placing a hand on the cover of my journals and saying things such as:

- Nobody may read these sacred pages without my permission.
- This journal is protected by positive energies.
- May this journal be protected by the power of the intentions placed upon it.
- Only energies with my best interest at heart are welcome here.
- Any negative energies I give to this book will be transmuted and healed.

STEP 5: SET YOUR INTENTION(S)

Setting intentions for how and what energies work with you is just as important as protecting the energy of your journal. If you only focus on the protection part, I have found the energy tends to get stuck. Remember we have the power of freewill. This means that both negative and positive energies can't help or influence without our permission. You can also write your intentions as positive affirmations if that feels good to you.

SET YOUR INTENTION FOR THIS JOURNAL:

Ex. I welcome the energy of abundance, self awareness, healing and prosperity.

STEP 6: TRACK YOUR RITUAL

I have gotten in my own flow for this ritual, but it can be hard to remember what you decided to do or say and what you may want to add or change next time when you first start a new spiritual practice like this. This space is to write out what you did for your anointing ritual so that you have it in a safe place in case you want to use it again.

CHAPTER *Four*

BREAK UP CHECKLIST

Here are some things to check off your list after a break up so that both you and the other person can navigate this process with clarity and respect.

01 CREATE SEPARATION & BOUNDARIES — DONE ☐

No matter who initiated the breakup, ending a relationship represents a conscious decision to change the relationship intimacy and/or remove each other from your lives in some way. Both parties must actively strive to create and maintain this separation. Establishing clear boundaries is crucial to avoid any confusion about the status of the relationship. The level of entanglement in the relationship will dictate the time required for a complete separation. If living together, it's advisable not to share the same room or bed. One of you may choose to stay with a friend temporarily. There must be a clear difference in the intimacy level of how you interact with each other both physically and emotionally. Take care not to fall into old habits. Doing so can cause confusion and prolong the process.

---

02 SET REASONBLE DEADLINES — DONE ☐

Set specific times to address any lingering issues and reasonable deadlines for resolution. The goal here is not to drag things out, have any excuses to remain in contact or use things as negotiating/bargaining chips.

---

03 FINAL EXCHANGE OF ITEMS — DONE ☐

Collect all items that you need to return to your ex and ask they do the same. Set one time to exchange and be done with it.

04 CLOSE OUT FINAL UNFINISHED BUISNESS

DONE ☐

Use the opportunity when exchanging final items to address any remaining unfinished business or loose ends. Use this time for any remaining necessary discussions. When contemplating the possibility of a future friendship, be mindful that taking time to heal and move on before initiating contact and friendship is crucial. Remaining friends with exes can be messy for both parties and any new romantic partners in your life. If you wish to keep the option open for a friendship down the road, consider communicating your intention to cut off all contact and remove each other from social media to facilitate the healing process. I don't recommend setting a specific deadline for reopening communication as your healing journey is yours and it can be nonlinear. You can always re-friend each other at a later date on social media when and if staying friends is right for you both and the time is right. Clearly expressing this boundary will help prevent any additional hurt feelings or confusion. However, it's essential to acknowledge that remaining friends might not always be possible, so prioritize personal growth and put healing first.

05 CEASE ALL CONTACT

DONE ☐

Having completed steps 1-4, there should be no need for you or your ex to contact each other. You cannot properly focus on healing if you are still involved with each other. Your future is not in your past. Consider deleting or blocking each other's phone numbers to prevent any inadvertent communication. By taking this precautionary measure, you can maintain the separation and focus on moving forward with your respective lives.

06 SOCIAL MEDIA CLEAN UP: BLOCK + UPDATE

DONE ☐

Block your ex on all social media platforms. Although it may seem harsh, blocking, rather than just unfriending or unfollowing, ensures that your ex won't randomly appear on your page or in suggestions. It also prevents both of you from keeping tabs on each other, allowing you to focus on moving forward without unnecessary distractions, reminders or misinterpretations.

Give thought to removing or archiving any couples pictures. Instead of deleting them, simply put them away where they won't be in sight and you won't come across them unexpectedly. You can decide what to do with them later when emotions are running less high. Consider removing or updating relationship statuses. Also, update or change your profile picture if necessary. By doing so, you can create a fresh start and avoid any reminders of the past relationship while presenting your current self to the online world.

07 REMOVE + AVOID TRIGGERS & FIGHT URGES

DONE ☐

Gather all the physical memorabilia associated with the relationship and store them in a box. To safeguard against impulsive actions, emotional outbursts or clinging to the past during your healing journey, consider asking a trusted friend to hold onto the box or store it somewhere safe but out of sight. Avoid places you know your ex frequents to minimize chances of running into them. Take the time to remove any songs from your playlist that remind you of the past relationship. Also, collect any pictures on your phone and store them in a designated folder, keeping them out of immediate view.

Resist the urge to contact your ex, stalk them on social media, or dwell on old memories, as these actions hinder the space needed for healing. You can't move on if you are clinging to the past. Avoid making sudden and drastic changes to your appearance until you've reached a more healed state. By following these steps, you can create a healthier environment for yourself and allow the healing process to unfold naturally.

---

08 GIVE YOURSELF TIME TO FEEL

DONE ☐

Regardless of whether the breakup brought relief or disappointment, it is crucial to allocate time to experience and process the multitude of emotions that accompany it. Alone and on your own terms. By working through these feelings, we can also bring closure to karmic cycles and debts. It's essential to acknowledge emotions, allowing yourself to feel them fully, but without getting overwhelmed or consumed by them. Finding a healthy balance in processing feelings empowers us to move forward and embrace the healing journey. Journaling is a great way to do this.

---

09 CREATE MOVEMENT

DONE ☐

Engaging in exercise acts as a natural mood elevator. Choose an activity you enjoy, one that gets you moving and encourages mindfulness. The movement doesn't always need to be a huge intensive workout. A simple walk is highly underrated and has proven to increase problem solving. If you're feeling restless, a leisurely hike can be beneficial. On the other hand, if your mind is racing, opt for an activity that requires attention but isn't overly thought-intensive.

10 GET SUPPORT

DONE ☐

Allocate time to be with the members of your inner circle and let them provide support and insight. However, be mindful not to overwhelm them with your emotions or burden them with excessive emotional labor. In certain breakups, professional help may be necessary. If you find yourself struggling to cope, don't hesitate to seek assistance from a trained professional. They can provide the guidance and support you need to navigate this challenging time effectively as well as give you additional tools to help you on your journey.

11 STAY SINGLE FOR AWHILE

DONE ☐

Even if you were the one to initiate the breakup, and it was a change you welcomed, refrain from hastily entering into a new relationship. Grant yourself the essential time for healing, reconnecting with your identity or reimagining yourself. Allow yourself a period to focus on your needs without factoring in the thoughts or expectations of another person. Ensure that when you decide to enter into a new relationship you are ready.

12 LEARN THE KARMIC LESSONS

DONE ☐

Take the opportunity to learn the karmic lessons from the relationship. Once you've given yourself some space and processed your emotions following the breakup, this step will be the most effective. The space will give you perspective to embark on the journey of introspection to evaluate the valuable lessons that the relationship has taught you. By doing so, you can gain deeper insights into yourself and your experiences, cultivating personal growth and understanding.

13 LOOK FORWARD TO THE FUTURE

DONE ☐

Take the time to explore and contemplate the new opportunities that await you in your single life. It's not just about romance; it could be something as simple as activities or interests you didn't have time for before but can now pursue. Embrace the chance to discover and enjoy the many possibilities that come with being single, and seize the moments that enhance your personal growth and fulfillment.

14 **GET CLOSURE** DONE ☐

Closure and forgiveness are not a gift bestowed upon us by someone else or achieved through someone else's apology. It is also not a dismissal of any wrong doing. It is an internal process that we grant ourselves by engaging in the necessary healing work. True closure emerges from within as we actively work through our emotions and experiences, allowing ourselves to find peace and resolution independently. It is the empowering ability we grant ourselves that liberates from the emotional and mental weight of an experience.

---

15 **REBUILD YOUR SELF CONFIDENCE, SELF WORTH & OVERALL SELF ESTEEM** DONE ☐

Embark on introspective efforts to reconstruct your confidence, rekindle your self-worth and build your overall self esteem. Through dedicated self-examination, nurturing self-care, and personal development, you can gradually unearth your inner resilience and inherent value. Keep in mind that healing is a gradual process; therefore, practice patience and self-compassion along the way. If your self-worth is solid, you might consider directing your attention toward cultivating self-confidence as a newly single individual by exploring, experimenting or rediscovering yourself.

---

16 **REALIGN YOUR GOALS** DONE ☐

For some of you, this may lead to putting yourself back out there, but it's crucial not to rush into a new relationship until you're genuinely ready. Take the time to reevaluate your romantic and other life goals. Align your reality and energy with what you wish to manifest. Allow yourself the space and readiness to attract the right connections and experiences in your life. Take your time and enjoy the process.

---

17 **INFUSE NEW ENERGY** DONE ☐

Create new habits, spiritual practices and routines that support your goals, personal healing and self confidence in positive ways. Usher in new energies by cleaning your space, reorganizing your space and/or moving furniture into a new set up in your home. This new energy can help you literally move into a new era of your life, feel more motivated and energized and release the old to make way for the new.

---

18 **FALL IN LOVE WITH YOU AGAIN** DONE ☐

CHAPTER *Five*

STARTING POINT

DATE: / /

Take a moment to evaluate where you are and how you are feeling. This evaluation is designed to give you insight into where you currently stand so you know what your starting point is.

REMIND YOURSELF OF YOUR INTENTION FOR THIS JOURNAL :

HOW DO YOU FEEL PHYSICALLY RIGHT NOW?

HOW DO YOU FEEL MENTALLY RIGHT NOW?

HOW DO YOU FEEL EMOTIONALLY RIGHT NOW?

HOW DO YOU FEEL SPIRITUALLY RIGHT NOW?

WHAT IS CONTRIBUTING TO HOW YOU FEEL PHYSICALLY?

WHAT IS CONTRIBUTING TO HOW YOU FEEL MENTALLY?

WHAT IS CONTRIBUTING TO HOW YOU FEEL EMOTIONALLY?

WHAT IS CONTRIBUTING TO HOW YOU FEEL SPIRITUALLY?

Rate Your Self Confidence

1 2 3 4 5 ___

No Confidence — Feeling Confident

Why did you give yourself this score?

What things contribute to your self confidence?

What things contribute to your lack of self confidence?

Rate Your Self Worth

1 2 3 4 5 ___

Not worthy — I Know My Worth

Why did you give yourself this score?

What things contribute to your self worth?

What things contribute to your lack of self worth?

Rate Your Value

1 2 3 4 5 ___

I Don't Feel Valuable — I Know My Value

Why did you give yourself this score?

What things contribute to your value?

What things contribute to feeling like you are less valuable?

FREE WRITE:

Free writing is a journaling practice that involves writing whatever comes to mind without judgment, evaluation, or a specific goal. This exercise allows thoughts and emotions to surface, enabling you to access your subconscious mind and declutter your thoughts. Often, we have a tendency to edit or filter our emotions and thoughts. This practice encourages you to be unfiltered, helping you gain a deeper insight into your thoughts and feelings. Utilize this space to jot down anything that crosses your mind. Keep writing until at least one page is filled. If you feel compelled, you can continue beyond that point; and stop whenever it feels right for you. I suggest filling at least one page because sometimes it takes a moment for the practice to take effect. It's acceptable to switch thoughts mid-sentence, write seeming nonsense, or follow streams of thought. Don't be concerned about spelling or directing the flow. Just write whatever needs to be expressed.

QUICK REFLECTION:

Reflecting on this exercise, did any profound realizations surface? Take a moment to jot down any insights about yourself, your emotions, or your thoughts for future reference. If this process didn't yield any new learnings or epiphanies, that's perfectly fine. Sometimes, the primary objective is to express and release rather than necessarily gain insights.

CHAPTER *Six*

A REMINDER YOU ARE LOVED & SUPPORTED

Support Comes In Various Ways & They Are All An Expression of Love

Going through a breakup might make you feel isolated, but that feeling of isolation is typically not an accurate depiction of reality. The individuals of our inner circle play a vital role as supporters and mentors, especially during challenging phases. They can share valuable wisdom, guidance and even provide healthy distractions.

Every individual within your inner circle brings a distinct approach to providing support, and support itself can manifest in diverse ways. Some friends are your go-to for a good laugh, while others are perfect for those deep, soul-searching conversations. While one friend might excel at offering problem-solving ideas, another may be better equipped to provide you with a place to stay for the night. Every form of support—be it emotional, mental, spiritual, or physical—brings its own unique contribution, yet each is an expression of love.

The right kind of support can play a pivotal role in aiding to the tranquility of the healing process while the wrong kind of support can introduce more distress. Recognizing the specific support that fits your needs and identifying the members of your support system who align best with that kind of support can alleviate stress, aid in coping, keep the energy of your relationships in balance, help you draw healthy boundaries and facilitate effective communication of your needs. This awareness enables intentional and purposeful allocation of energy in your healing journey while preventing unrealistic or unfair expectations of your friends and family.

4 SUPPORT STYLES

Outlined below are four styles of support and various ways in which they may manifest. While these support styles often intertwine, it's possible for certain friends or family members to predominantly exhibit specific support styles.

Emotional

Emotional support focuses on your emotional wellbeing, managing mood and your sense of belonging.

Some Manifestations:

- Listening with empathy.
- Physical gestures of affection.
- Giving undivided attention.
- Acknowledging and validating emotions.
- Being physically present.
- Making someone laugh.

Mental

Mental support focuses on your mental wellbeing, positive decision making and rational thinking.

Some Manifestations:

- Reminding someone of their strengths.
- Boosting someone's confidence.
- Problem solving, providing practical advice or resources & planning.
- Helping to motivate.
- Challenging limiting beliefs.
- Providing accountability

Physical

Physical support focuses on financial stability, material support. and physical wellbeing.

Some Manifestations:

- Financial support such as lending money or paying a bill.
- Offering to drive someone somewhere.
- Providing meals or ensuring basic needs are being met.
- Lending a hand, running errands, providing childcare or other forms of help.
- Physical gestures of affection.

Spiritual

Spiritual support focuses on your spiritual wellbeing and connectedness, grounding and being present in the moment.

Some Manifestations:

- Having deep, spiritual conversations or giving spiritual advice.
- Doing something creative together.
- Practicing mindfulness.
- Reminding someone to live in the moment.
- Engaging in shared spiritual activities.

Healthy Support Includes Holding Accountability

Over giving is not healthy support. When support falls into over giving territory, it becomes enabling.

Remember it's important to keep in mind that your inner circle is there to provide support, not to shoulder the burden of emotional labor or take on all responsibilities in which you should be accountable. While it's okay for them to help lighten the load temporarily and within reasonable boundaries, ultimately, you're still responsible for that which is yours. It's neither fair nor healthy to expect your support system to bear that weight for you.

While it's acceptable to discuss the breakup and seek support from others, be mindful not to overwhelm, engage in repetitive discussions, or place unfair expectations that should be your responsibility. These behaviors can be draining on your inner circle and cause them to create distance from you in order to maintain healthy boundaries for themselves. Maintaining balance is key—remember to inquire about their lives as well and try not to allow your interactions to fall completely into the negative. Avoid a sole focus on yourself and your issues by remembering to offer healthy support to your inner circle in return.

Evaluate Your Support System

Take a moment to take stock of the members of your inner circle. This list can include friends and family, but don't forget to include members of your spirit team (such as the universe, guides, ancestors, etc.) as well as any professionals in your support system such as life coaches or therapists. Use this list as a reminder that you are loved and supported. Remember, the support and love you have for self counts.

Use this list to remind you who you can lean on when you need some added support or a bit of fun. Make some quick notes of the kind of support each relationship is more naturally inclined to provide.

Inner Circle Member	Ways They Show Support

Inner Circle Member	Ways They Show Support

A LETTER FROM YOUR BEST FRIEND, YOU

Draft a letter to yourself, assuming the role of your own best friend. Consider what you would say to yourself in this moment, and what guidance, support and counsel you would offer. This activity aims to connect with your inner guidance and serve as a reminder that you are your own source of support.

CHAPTER *Seven*

RAISE YOUR VIBRATION

Energy creates energy and energy is contagious. Allowing negativity to dominate your life will only attract more of the same, while embracing positivity as your focal point will draw in additional positive energy. It's perfectly acceptable to experience and acknowledge the array of emotions that accompany a breakup. Yet, there are times when we find ourselves stuck, unmotivated, or in a low mood. In these moments, we often need a boost of positive energy to raise our vibration. While our inner circle is an excellent source of support, it is important to master the art of raising our vibration independently. Here are some ways to boost your mood. Keep this list handy for those times when you're in need of a lift. This section will also help you put some of this into practice.

MEDITATION	Energy cleansing, grounding or general meditation can help raise your vibrational frequency.
FREE WRITE	Free writing can effectively declutter your mind and allow you to express all your thoughts and feelings freely, removing negative blocks.
LISTEN TO UPBEAT MUSIC	Music is a powerful tool that can heal and shift our mood. Certain frequencies are even known to reduce stress and promote calm.
PRACTICE GRATITUDE	Were you aware that practicing gratitude can also alleviate stress? The human brain cannot simultaneously feel gratitude and anxiety, which makes gratitude an effective technique for managing stress, worry and anxiety. Start by listing some things you are grateful for.

LAUGH	Have you ever heard that saying laughter is the best medicine? That is because laughter releases feel good hormones in our brains that elevate mood.
UNPLUG	Taking a break from the constant buzz of social media and content/media consumption. It can have a profound impact on our energy. Unplugging allows us to reconnect with the present moment, free from the distractions, chaos and stress that drains our processing power. By stepping away from screens and immersing ourselves in real-life experiences, we create space for introspection, self-care, and genuine connections. This intentional break rejuvenates our spirit, elevates our vibration, and invites a sense of calm and clarity back into our lives.
MOVE	Moving your body is an excellent stress-reliever and can significantly elevate your vibration by releasing endorphins, boosting your mood, and increasing your overall energy levels. Bust out some dance moves, go for a walk, or engage in a workout.
CATCH SOME RAYS	Many spiritual practitioners believe the sun is healing. Sunlight also stimulates the production of serotonin, the "feel-good" hormone, promoting a sense of well-being and boosting our mood. The sun also helps in the production of vitamin D which affects mood and health. 10-30 minutes of unfiltered sunlight can do a world of good.
AFFIRMATIONS	Writing affirmations help not only to challenge negative and limiting beliefs, it can assist in raising your vibrational energy and help create new neural pathways that can later streamline manifestation.

ASK THE UNIVERSE OR YOUR SPIRIT GUIDES FOR HELP	Remember that you are not alone. The universe loves and supports you. Reach out to the universe and your spiritual guides for assistance. Ask for guidance, and be open to receiving their supportive energies, which can amplify your efforts to raise your vibration and attract positivity into your life.
CONNECT WITH NATURE	Nature has a unique ability to soothe your mind, body, and soul. Spend time outdoors appreciating nature, whether it's walking through a botanical garden, a hike in the woods, or simply sitting by a serene body of water. Spirit animals may appear.
CLEAN YOUR SPACE	Clearing both your physical and energetic space can have a profound impact on elevating your vibrational energy. Declutter and tidy up your physical surroundings. A clean and organized space can create a sense of calm and tranquility, allowing positive energy to flow freely. Next, consider energetically cleansing your space using methods like sprinkling salt, visualization, burning herbs or using crystals known for their cleansing properties. Rearranging your space can also infuse new energy and help in reducing triggers.
EAT HEALTHY & DRINK WATER	Eating healthy and staying hydrated can keep your energy levels high and your physical body healthy.
SURROUND YOURSELF WITH POSITIVITY	Ensure any content you are consuming is positive in nature, spend time doing things and spending time with people that make you feel happy and loved.

FREE WRITE

Free writing is a journaling practice that involves writing whatever comes to mind without judgment, evaluation, or a specific goal. This exercise allows thoughts and emotions to surface, enabling you to access your subconscious mind and declutter your thoughts. Often, we have a tendency to edit or filter our emotions and thoughts. This practice encourages you to be unfiltered, helping you gain a deeper insight into your thoughts and feelings. Utilize this space to jot down anything that crosses your mind. Keep writing until at least one page is filled. If you feel compelled, you can continue beyond that point; and stop whenever it feels right for you. I suggest filling at least one page because sometimes it takes a moment for the practice to take effect. It's acceptable to switch thoughts mid-sentence, write seeming nonsense, or follow streams of thought. Don't be concerned about spelling or directing the flow. Just write whatever needs to be expressed.

Extra Space or Come Back Later

Use these next few pages as additional space or feel free to come back to this section when you need to repeat this exercise.

PRACTICE GRATITUDE

Use Gratitude To Shift Your Energy

Scientific evidence supports the idea that individuals who regularly practice gratitude lead more fulfilling and happy lives. Engaging in gratitude can provide a fresh perspective, especially in challenging or disappointing moments. This practice trains your brain to focus on creativity instead of complaints and solutions rather than problems, developing a more positive mindset. And remember, expressing gratitude for what you have attracts more reasons to be thankful from the universe.

These next two exercises are designed to help you learn two types of energy shifting gratitude practices that I implemented into my daily spiritual practices many years ago.

Gratitude Warm Up

Let's start with a quick warm up to get in the right frame of mind. List 6 things you are grateful for.

I'M GRATEFUL FOR...

______

______

______

______

______

______

GENERAL ENERGY SHIFTING GRATITUDE

This gratitude practice is excellent for those new to the practice and proves beneficial when transitioning from states of anxiety or worry to a more positive mindset as the brain can not focus on both simultaneously. The effectiveness is heightened by specifying not just what you're grateful for but also why. This approach facilitates a deeper connection, understanding and immersion, helping you identify the root energies that resonate most with you. Root energies are the deeper overall underlying energy of an experience or thing. An example of a root energy would be when people desire wealth, what they often really want is freedom.

If you encounter difficulty, begin with simple things that are often overlooked. Whether it's having the gift of sight or a comfortable bed to sleep in, acknowledging these basics can be a starting point. Once you overcome the initial challenge, you'll discover that finding reasons to be grateful comes easy.

Engaging in the practice of gratitude triggers the release of chemicals in your brain associated with feelings of happiness and positivity. By developing a habitual gratitude practice, your brain develops a natural tendency to actively seek out more things to be grateful for, leading to an increased release of these joyful chemicals. In essence, it trains your brain to consistently embrace and focus on positivity, making you a magnet for positive energy.

I'M GRATEFUL FOR...	BECAUSE...

GENERAL ENERGY SHIFTING GRATITUDE

Extra Space or Come Back Later

Use these next few pages as additional space or feel free to come back to this section when you need another pick me up.

I'M GRATEFUL FOR...	BECAUSE...

GENERAL ENERGY SHIFTING GRATITUDE

I'M GRATEFUL FOR...	BECAUSE...

GENERAL ENERGY SHIFTING GRATITUDE

I'M GRATEFUL FOR...	BECAUSE...

GRATITUDE FOR NEW PERSPECTIVES

Now that you've learned a general gratitude practice, let's expand on your new skills. While this section may pose a greater challenge, it's designed to help you discover gratitude even when positivity seems elusive, provide reference points and instill confidence in your ability to be resilient.

The emotional intensity of difficult times is subjective; what one individual may perceive as an impossible situation could be considered difficult but surmountable by another.When we find ourselves fixating intently on a particular moment in time, the associated pain or suffering can feel all-encompassing. Comparing the present situation to other hardships faced in the past can effectively reduce the perceived enormity of the challenges being confronted and remind you of what you have already overcome.

One thing that truly irks me is when people claim, "My trauma or my pain made me stronger." It's important to recognize that your trauma or pain didn't make you stronger. The things that break you are not what makes you strong. Your strength and resilience arise from the conscious choice to be strong and resilient.

In this exercise, I encourage you to identify aspects of your current situation to be grateful for and find gratitude in another challenging moment in your life you already overcame. The goal of this exercise isn't to appreciate wrongdoing or the people and circumstances that caused pain. Instead, it's about uncovering blessings in disguise or glimpses of light in the darkness. Take time to reflect on the two situations and use the reference points to widen your perspective on your current circumstances.

Here is an example of a break up from my past and the difficult situation of my brother's passing to give you a real example of this exercise. I used the passing of my brother as an example because I want to show you how there is light to be found in even the darkest of circumstances. Sometimes it takes a bit of looking.

Gratitude For New Pespective Example:

DIFFICULT SITUATION:

I had to break up with my first love not because I didn't love him but because he wasn't good for me.

I'M GRATEFUL FOR...

Having the strength to honor my needs

BECAUSE...

My happiness and peace of mind matter

I'M GRATEFUL FOR...

Knowing myself well enough to not lose myself in a relationship

BECAUSE...

Being my most authentic self in a romantic relationship is a priority for me

I'M GRATEFUL FOR...

The feelings of discomfort in my body that told me I wasn't where I belonged

BECAUSE...

these feelings, though uncomfortable, were messages from my intuition and higher self

I'M GRATEFUL FOR...

The opportunity life provides for things to end and new things to begin

BECAUSE...

It means I am never stuck in one place or one situation forever

ANOTHER DIFFICULT SITUATION:

My brother died at age 21

I'M GRATEFUL FOR...

The choice I made to leave Los Angeles when I did even though I didn't want to

BECAUSE...

I didn't know it a the time, but moving home allowed me to spend time with my brother I otherwise would not have had before he died

I'M GRATEFUL FOR...

The support I had from friends and family

BECAUSE...

the support helped share the emotional weight of the loss and keep his memory alive

I'M GRATEFUL FOR...

The fact that my brother's loss was not the first major loss I experienced

BECAUSE...

as morbid as it may sound, I was better prepared for how to deal with such deep rooted grief

I'M GRATEFUL FOR...

All the little, seemingly insignificant moments I had with my brother while he was alive

BECAUSE...

It taught me how important it is to be present and how important those little moment really are

Gratitude For New Pespective Example:

COMPARE THE TWO SITUATIONS & REFLECT:

The loss of my brother and a breakup with a boyfriend are experiences that, to me, don't equate in terms of emotional impact. If faced with a breakup now, I'm inclined to believe that I could navigate the healing process more confidently. Even though the breakup was undeniably challenging at the time, reflecting on it in the context of other life events allows me to recognize that I've endured and triumphed over far more difficult and painful circumstances.

It's not about diminishing the significance of the breakup but acknowledging the resilience I've cultivated through a variety of life challenges, which in turn provides a valuable perspective on the capacity for healing and growth. By comparing the break up to a broader spectrum of experiences, it becomes a pivotal part of a larger narrative of overcoming adversity, reinforcing the belief that I possess the strength to face and overcome challenges, no matter how difficult they may seem in the moment.

GRATITUDE FOR NEW PERSPECTIVES EXERCISE

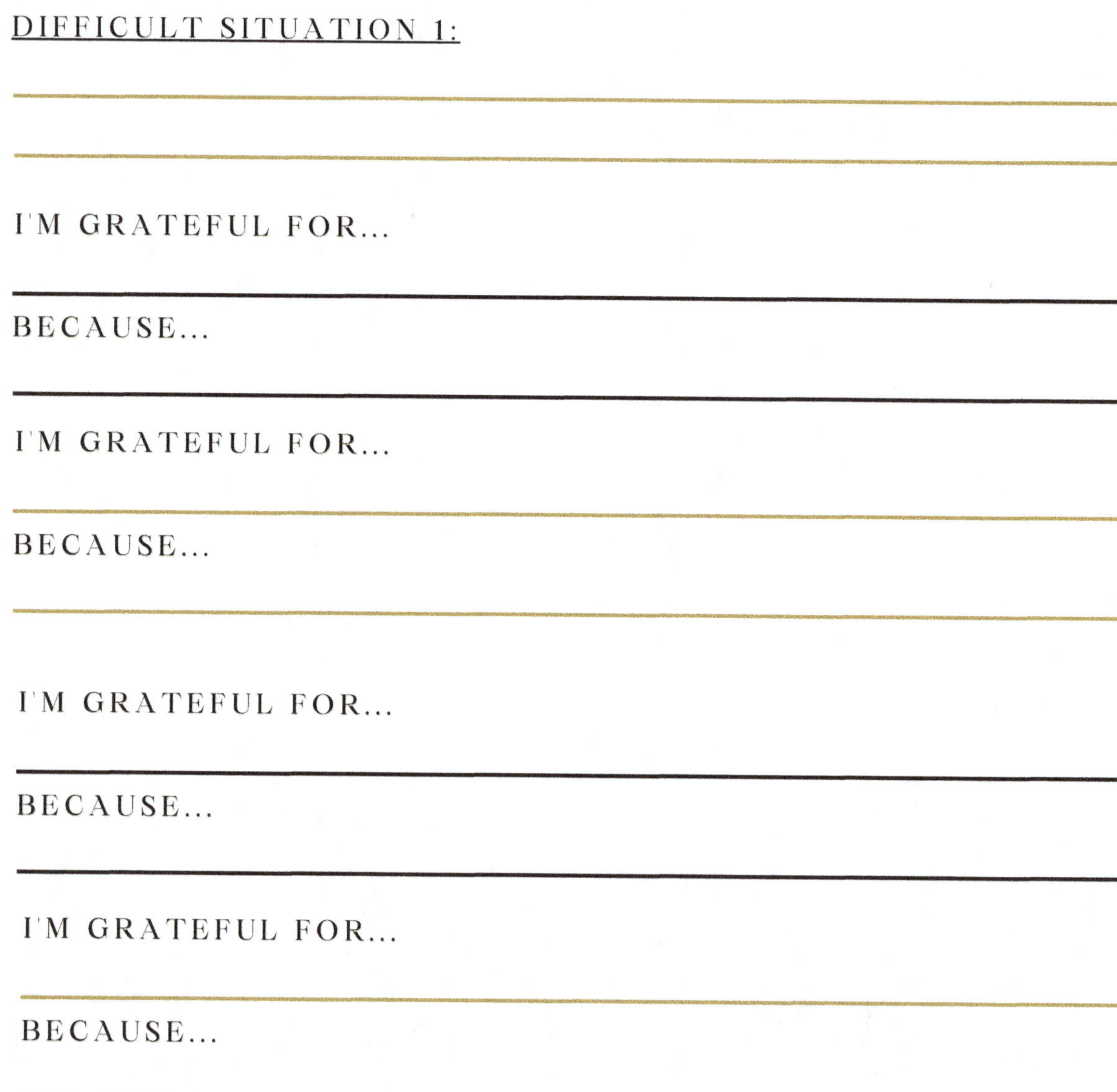

DIFFICULT SITUATION 2:

I'M GRATEFUL FOR...

BECAUSE...

I'M GRATEFUL FOR...

BECAUSE...

I'M GRATEFUL FOR...

BECAUSE...

I'M GRATEFUL FOR...

BECAUSE...

COMPARE THE TWO SITUATIONS & REFLECT:

Extra Space or Come Back Later

Use these next few pages as additional space or feel free to come back to this section when you need to repeat this practice.

DIFFICULT SITUATION 1:

I'M GRATEFUL FOR...

BECAUSE...

I'M GRATEFUL FOR...

BECAUSE...

I'M GRATEFUL FOR...

BECAUSE...

I'M GRATEFUL FOR...

BECAUSE...

DIFFICULT SITUATION 2:

I'M GRATEFUL FOR...

BECAUSE...

I'M GRATEFUL FOR...

BECAUSE...

I'M GRATEFUL FOR...

BECAUSE...

I'M GRATEFUL FOR...

BECAUSE...

COMPARE THE TWO SITUATIONS & REFLECT:

GRATITUDE CHALLENGE

The practice of gratitude profoundly transformed my life. First, I used it as a means to manage my anxiety but soon my practice expanded into a daily routine that is a pivotal part of my daily spiritual practices. It still astounds me how such a small habit could yield such a significant impact. As I started incorporating gratitude into my routine, I noticed a shift in my perspective, a change in my energy, and a corresponding transformation in the world around me.

I challenge you to practice gratitude every day for two weeks and track how you feel. See if making gratitude a part of your daily routine has the same profound impact in your life as it had on mine.

Feel free to take part in this challenge as you continue to move through this book. Although I highly recommend trying this challenge, as it is designed to help elevate your mood, provide a new perspective, and cultivate new healthy habits, unlike some other sections in this book, you do not need to complete the challenge before moving forward.

DAY 1

DATE: / /

Morning Routine

Start your day by listing 3 things you are grateful for. Write them below or say them in your head. I suggest writing them down so you can remember what you wrote when you go back to reflect on your practice.

I'M GRATEFUL FOR...	BECAUSE...

Evening Routine

End your day by listing 3 things you are grateful for. It can be things from the day itself or unrelated. Try not to list the same things you listed in your morning practice. Write them below or say them in your head. I suggest writing them down so you can remember what you wrote when you go back to reflect on your practice.

I'M GRATEFUL FOR...	BECAUSE...

DAY 2

DATE: / /

Morning Routine

Start your day by listing 3 things you are grateful for.

I'M GRATEFUL FOR... BECAUSE...

Rate Your Sleep Last Night

1 2 3 4 5 ___

What Sleep? Like A Baby

Why did you give yourself this score?

Evening Routine

End your day by listing 3 things you are grateful for. It can be things from the day itself or unrelated. Try not to list the same things you listed in your morning practice.

I'M GRATEFUL FOR... BECAUSE...

Rate Your Mood After Your Gratitude Practices

1 2 3 4 5 ___

Feeling Very Negative Feeling Very Positive

Why did you give yourself this score?

How long did the effects last?

Rate Your Overall Mood Today

1 2 3 4 5 ___

Feeling Very Negative Feeling Very Positive

Why did you give yourself this score?

DAY 3

DATE: / /

Morning Routine

Start your day by listing 3 things you are grateful for.

I'M GRATEFUL FOR...

BECAUSE...

Rate Your Sleep Last Night

1 2 3 4 5 —

What Sleep? Like A Baby

Why did you give yourself this score?

Evening Routine

End your day by listing 3 things you are grateful for. It can be things from the day itself or unrelated. Try not to list the same things you listed in your morning practice.

I'M GRATEFUL FOR...

BECAUSE...

Rate Your Mood After Your Gratitude Practices

1 2 3 4 5 —

Feeling Very Negative Feeling Very Positive

Why did you give yourself this score?

How long did the effects last?

Rate Your Overall Mood Today

1 2 3 4 5 —

Feeling Very Negative Feeling Very Positive

Why did you give yourself this score?

DAY 4

DATE: / /

Morning Routine

Start your day by listing 3 things you are grateful for.

I'M GRATEFUL FOR... BECAUSE...

Rate Your Sleep Last Night

1 2 3 4 5 ___

What Sleep? Like A Baby

Why did you give yourself this score?

Evening Routine

End your day by listing 3 things you are grateful for. It can be things from the day itself or unrelated. Try not to list the same things you listed in your morning practice.

I'M GRATEFUL FOR... BECAUSE...

Rate Your Mood After Your Gratitude Practices

1 2 3 4 5 ___

Feeling Very Negative Feeling Very Positive

Why did you give yourself this score?

How long did the effects last?

Rate Your Overall Mood Today

1 2 3 4 5 ___

Feeling Very Negative Feeling Very Positive

Why did you give yourself this score?

DAY 5

DATE: / /

Morning Routine

Start your day by listing 3 things you are grateful for.

I'M GRATEFUL FOR... BECAUSE...

Rate Your Sleep Last Night

1 2 3 4 5 —

What Sleep? Like A Baby

Why did you give yourself this score?

Evening Routine

End your day by listing 3 things you are grateful for. It can be things from the day itself or unrelated. Try not to list the same things you listed in your morning practice.

I'M GRATEFUL FOR... BECAUSE...

Rate Your Mood After Your Gratitude Practices

1 2 3 4 5 —

Feeling Very Negative Feeling Very Positive

Why did you give yourself this score?

How long did the effects last?

Rate Your Overall Mood Today

1 2 3 4 5 —

Feeling Very Negative Feeling Very Positive

Why did you give yourself this score?

DAY 6

DATE: / /

Morning Routine

Start your day by listing 3 things you are grateful for.

I'M GRATEFUL FOR...

BECAUSE...

Rate Your Sleep Last Night

1 2 3 4 5

What Sleep? Like A Baby

Why did you give yourself this score?

Evening Routine

End your day by listing 3 things you are grateful for. It can be things from the day itself or unrelated. Try not to list the same things you listed in your morning practice.

I'M GRATEFUL FOR...

BECAUSE...

Rate Your Mood After Your Gratitude Practices

1 2 3 4 5

Feeling Very Negative Feeling Very Positive

Why did you give yourself this score?

How long did the effects last?

Rate Your Overall Mood Today

1 2 3 4 5

Feeling Very Negative Feeling Very Positive

Why did you give yourself this score?

DAY 7

DATE: / /

Morning Routine

Start your day by listing 3 things you are grateful for.

I'M GRATEFUL FOR... BECAUSE...

Rate Your Sleep Last Night

1 2 3 4 5 ___

What Sleep? Like A Baby

Why did you give yourself this score?

Evening Routine

End your day by listing 3 things you are grateful for. It can be things from the day itself or unrelated. Try not to list the same things you listed in your morning practice.

I'M GRATEFUL FOR... BECAUSE...

Rate Your Mood After Your Gratitude Practices

1 2 3 4 5 ___

Feeling Very Negative Feeling Very Positive

Why did you give yourself this score?

How long did the effects last?

Rate Your Overall Mood Today

1 2 3 4 5 ___

Feeling Very Negative Feeling Very Positive

Why did you give yourself this score?

DAY 8

DATE: / /

Morning Routine

Start your day by listing 3 things you are grateful for.

I'M GRATEFUL FOR...

BECAUSE...

Rate Your Sleep Last Night

1 2 3 4 5 ___

What Sleep? Like A Baby

Why did you give yourself this score?

Evening Routine

End your day by listing 3 things you are grateful for. It can be things from the day itself or unrelated. Try not to list the same things you listed in your morning practice.

I'M GRATEFUL FOR...

BECAUSE...

Rate Your Mood After Your Gratitude Practices

1 2 3 4 5 ___

Feeling Very Negative Feeling Very Positive

Why did you give yourself this score?

How long did the effects last?

Rate Your Overall Mood Today

1 2 3 4 5 ___

Feeling Very Negative Feeling Very Positive

Why did you give yourself this score?

DAY 9

DATE: / /

Morning Routine

Start your day by listing 3 things you are grateful for.

I'M GRATEFUL FOR... BECAUSE...

Rate Your Sleep Last Night

1 2 3 4 5 —

What Sleep? Like A Baby

Why did you give yourself this score?

Evening Routine

End your day by listing 3 things you are grateful for. It can be things from the day itself or unrelated. Try not to list the same things you listed in your morning practice.

I'M GRATEFUL FOR... BECAUSE...

Rate Your Mood After Your Gratitude Practices

1 2 3 4 5 —

Feeling Very Negative Feeling Very Positive

Why did you give yourself this score?

How long did the effects last?

Rate Your Overall Mood Today

1 2 3 4 5 —

Feeling Very Negative Feeling Very Positive

Why did you give yourself this score?

DAY 10

DATE: / /

Morning Routine

Start your day by listing 3 things you are grateful for.

I'M GRATEFUL FOR...

BECAUSE...

Rate Your Sleep Last Night

1 2 3 4 5 —

What Sleep? Like A Baby

Why did you give yourself this score?

Evening Routine

End your day by listing 3 things you are grateful for. It can be things from the day itself or unrelated. Try not to list the same things you listed in your morning practice.

I'M GRATEFUL FOR...

BECAUSE...

Rate Your Mood After Your Gratitude Practices

1 2 3 4 5 —

Feeling Very Negative Feeling Very Positive

Why did you give yourself this score?

How long did the effects last?

Rate Your Overall Mood Today

1 2 3 4 5 —

Feeling Very Negative Feeling Very Positive

Why did you give yourself this score?

DAY 11

DATE: / /

Morning Routine

Start your day by listing 3 things you are grateful for.

I'M GRATEFUL FOR... BECAUSE...

Rate Your Sleep Last Night

1 2 3 4 5 —

What Sleep? Like A Baby

Why did you give yourself this score?

Evening Routine

End your day by listing 3 things you are grateful for. It can be things from the day itself or unrelated. Try not to list the same things you listed in your morning practice.

I'M GRATEFUL FOR... BECAUSE...

Rate Your Mood After Your Gratitude Practices

1 2 3 4 5 —

Feeling Very Negative Feeling Very Positive

Why did you give yourself this score?

How long did the effects last?

Rate Your Overall Mood Today

1 2 3 4 5 —

Feeling Very Negative Feeling Very Positive

Why did you give yourself this score?

DAY 12

DATE: / /

Morning Routine

Start your day by listing 3 things you are grateful for.

I'M GRATEFUL FOR...

BECAUSE...

Rate Your Sleep Last Night

1 2 3 4 5 ___

What Sleep? Like A Baby

Why did you give yourself this score?

Evening Routine

End your day by listing 3 things you are grateful for. It can be things from the day itself or unrelated. Try not to list the same things you listed in your morning practice.

I'M GRATEFUL FOR...

BECAUSE...

Rate Your Mood After Your Gratitude Practices

1 2 3 4 5 ___

Feeling Very Negative Feeling Very Positive

Why did you give yourself this score?

How long did the effects last?

Rate Your Overall Mood Today

1 2 3 4 5 ___

Feeling Very Negative Feeling Very Positive

Why did you give yourself this score?

DAY 13

DATE: / /

Morning Routine

Start your day by listing 3 things you are grateful for.

I'M GRATEFUL FOR...	BECAUSE...

Rate Your Sleep Last Night

1 2 3 4 5 ___

What Sleep? — Like A Baby

Why did you give yourself this score?

Evening Routine

End your day by listing 3 things you are grateful for. It can be things from the day itself or unrelated. Try not to list the same things you listed in your morning practice.

I'M GRATEFUL FOR...	BECAUSE...

Rate Your Mood After Your Gratitude Practices

1 2 3 4 5 ___

Feeling Very Negative — Feeling Very Positive

Why did you give yourself this score?

How long did the effects last?

Rate Your Overall Mood Today

1 2 3 4 5 ___

Feeling Very Negative — Feeling Very Positive

Why did you give yourself this score?

DAY 14

DATE: / /

Morning Routine

Start your day by listing 3 things you are grateful for.

I'M GRATEFUL FOR... BECAUSE...

Rate Your Sleep Last Night

1 2 3 4 5 ___

What Sleep? Like A Baby

Why did you give yourself this score?

Evening Routine

End your day by listing 3 things you are grateful for. It can be things from the day itself or unrelated. Try not to list the same things you listed in your morning practice.

I'M GRATEFUL FOR... BECAUSE...

Rate Your Mood After Your Gratitude Practices

1 2 3 4 5 ___

Feeling Very Negative Feeling Very Positive

Why did you give yourself this score?

How long did the effects last?

Rate Your Overall Mood Today

1 2 3 4 5 ___

Feeling Very Negative Feeling Very Positive

Why did you give yourself this score?

Challenge Reflection

Mood

Did you notice any changes in your mood over the two weeks of practicing gratitude? If so, how did gratitude impact your mood?

Did you notice any changes in your thought cycles or self talk over the two weeks of practicing gratitude? If so, how did gratitude impact your mindset?

What did you find easier during or after this practice?

How did your gratitude list change over the course of this practice?

Where there any other things you noticed or any other synchronicities that became clear to you during this challenge? If so, what were they?

Sleep

How did this challenge effect your sleep?

Revelations

Did you come to any revelations or did you learn anything about yourself through this challenge? If so, what were the revelations or what did you learn?

Free write anything that comes to mind about this challenge that was not covered in the rest of this reflection.

If you enjoyed this challenge how can you put gratitude into your daily practices in a way that works best for you? Are there things you would change?

AFFIRMATIONS

Some Affirmations For When You Feel Down

Affirmations are empowering statements spoken in the present tense to counteract negative or self-sabotaging thoughts. You can also write affirmations in the present tense of something you desire as if it has already happened to bring manifestations from the spiritual to the physical world. You can say these affirmations out loud, write them down in the provided space, modify them, or even contribute to this list. It is important that the affirmations you use feel convincing and right to you.

Sometimes it also helps to write and read them out loud. Choose what deeply resonates with you and feel free to disregard what doesn't align with your needs and intentions.

- I am loved and supported.
- I am not alone.
- I understand this pain will pass.
- I am here for myself.
- I am fully healed mind, body and soul.
- I welcome self understanding into my life.
- It is safe & okay to ask for help or support.
- I am whole.
- I see better days are right around the corner.
- I am healing.
- I feel happy and joyous.
- I speak healing into existence.
- I love and accept myself for who I am.
- I see the love that surrounds me.

Extra Space or Come Back Later

Use these next few pages as additional space or feel free to come back to this section when you need another pick me up.

ASK THE UNIVERSE & YOUR GUIDES FOR HELP

A resource that is available to everyone but that is often forgotten or overlooked is the support from your spirit team. Your spirit team consists of your spirit guides, angels, ancestors, friend or family who have passed on, the universal energies, your higher self, intuition and the ascended masters. Your higher self is your soul and/or divine spirit. Seeking assistance from your spirit team can be beneficial, especially when you're feeling down, you need support or you need guidance.

One thing to keep in mind is each of us was given the power of free will. This means that you may have a team of spirit guides, ancestors or the universe itself ready to offer help, but they require your permission to intervene. In short, you must **ask** for their help.

Some ways you can communicate with your guides and/or the universe is through prayer, writing a letter, engaging in meditation, or speaking to your guides/the universe out loud. Each of these communication methods is effective, so experiment with them to discover what works best for you.

A good practice to adopt is to ensure that, regardless of the method of communication you use, you begin your communication with the name(s) of the entity or entities you are addressing. Not only is this a common courtesy but it helps to create spiritual boundaries, ensure your message is sent to the correct entity and that entity knows you are speaking to them. Giving thanks is also a great way to start a conversation and expresses gratitude for what you have been given. You can also ask for specific signs or synchronicities that have a certain meaning to you or ask for more clarity on a message.

As a reference or template, here's an example of some written letter prayers that I use, which you can adapt to suit your needs.

LETTER TO SPIRIT EXAMPLES

A General Letter

Dear Universe, Spirit Guides, Allies & Ancestors,

Thank you for the miracles and blessings you have given me. Thank you for the ongoing guidance that has been sent and continues to come my way. Please continue to send me clear and gentle signs to guide me on my path. Please direct my thoughts, feelings, and perspectives towards my highest timeline and purpose. Thank you.

For Healing

Dear Members of My Spirit Team,

Thank you for the miracles and blessings you have given me. Thank you for the ongoing guidance that has been sent and continues to come my way. Please continue to send me clear and gentle signs to guide me on my path. Please direct my thoughts, feelings, and perspectives towards healing. I ask that you lead me towards that which will help with my healing journey and help to transmute all negative energies. Thank you.

For Clarity

Dear Universe, Spirit Guides, Allies & Ancestors,

Thank you for the miracles and blessings you have given me. Please send me a red cardinal bird as a reassuring sign of your presence. I ask that you send me a clear and gentle sign that will guide me towards the next steps on my journey and give me clarity as to what I should put my focus into. Thank you.

ASK THE UNIVERSE & YOUR GUIDES FOR HELP

Use this section to write your own prayers or letters to your spirit team.

TO SLEEP OR NOT TO SLEEP

When emotions are running high, your sleep can go one of two ways. Either it plays hard to get, leaving you tossing and turning, or you end up in a constant tiredness loop, making you hit the snooze button more than usual. Sleep is like a superhero for your health, wellbeing and mood, but when it decides to take a detour, it adds an extra layer to the stress you're already dealing with emotionally.

This section is all about finding some tricks to help your sleep, whether you're oversleeping or stuck in the can't-sleep club. This is by no means a complete list, but may give you some ideas you haven't considered. Do what is best for you and your body.

The Can't-Sleep Club: Tips, Tricks & Stress Management

01 REMOVE DISTRACTIONS

Although television and social media scrolling can certainly pass the time, the blue light from electronics has been scientifically proven to interrupt our internal clocks. Eliminating all activities involving blue light either when preparing for sleep or one to two hours before bedtime can significantly impact the quality of your sleep.

02 HERBAL OR DECAF TEAS & WARM DRINKS

Sipping on a soothing warm beverage like tea or even lemon water can be a nice way to unwind before bedtime. Herbal teas, such as chamomile, lavender or valerian root, are especially effective in reducing stress and promoting a restful night's sleep.

03 ESSENTIAL OILS

Research suggests Aromatherapy is great for reducing stress and improving sleep. Find a relaxing essential oil and fill your bedroom with relaxing scents. Side note: some essential oils can be harmful to pets so do your research.

04 BATHS & JACUZZIS

Indulging in a warm or hot water soak can work wonders to ease muscle tension. Whether you have access to a jacuzzi or opt for a hot bath, the benefits are substantial. If a bathtub or jacuzzi isn't an option, a hot shower can provide similar effects. Enhance muscle relaxation by adding Epsom salt to your bath, and if you have sensitive skin, choose a fragrance-free option.

05 ADAPTOGENS

Adaptogens are underrated.

Adaptogens often fly under the radar, and I wish more people were aware of their transformative potential. These remarkable herbs have been a game-changer in my life, offering a multitude of incredible benefits.

What are adaptogens?

Adaptogens are herbs, roots and plants that support the body in stress management and immune system fortification. They can help in reducing the stress hormone cortisol, assist your adrenal glands in functioning more effectively, calm your nervous system, balance hormones, and improving sleep. Particularly beneficial if you're experiencing brain fog or consuming high levels of caffeine, these potent herbs can offer significant assistance.

Taking adaptogens.

There's a diverse array of excellent and cost-effective supplements available, presented in various forms such as pills, drops & drinks.

06 STRETCHING

Stretching is not only fabulous for your body, but it can help relax your muscles. Stretching for ten to fifteen minutes before bed can get your body more relaxed and ready for sleep.

07 EXERCISE

Engaging in exercise helps release excess or pent-up energy. Whether it's an intense workout to induce tiredness, a walk to release energy or a calming activity like sleep yoga to relax the body and promote drowsiness, all can be beneficial. Side note: Some people find exercise gives them more energy and actually makes sleep more difficult immediately after a work out. Honor the best timing for you and your body.

08 SLEEP MUSIC & FREQUENCIES

Did you know our bodies respond to the different frequencies of music and those frequencies can actually affect our body on a biological level? Using sleep music or specific sleep frequencies can help relax the body, help you fall asleep faster and improve your sleep. Some frequencies are even tailored for healing during sleep, and you can find dedicated playlists for these on most music streaming services.

Side note: You may want to play around with different sounds, music or frequencies as some will work better for you than others. It is worth mentioning that if you have experienced trauma, certain frequencies or music can cause lucid dreaming, strange dreams or even nightmares.

09 JOURNALING

As you have already learned, gratitude is a great way to reduce stress and improve sleep. However, journaling and free writing can also be effective in reducing stress and clearing your mind before bed. Taking a few moments to plan for the following day or to write down any fears, worries, and anxieties has been shown to reduce stress and improve sleep.

10 MEDITATION

General meditation is effective in reducing stress and improving mental clarity. However, you can also use meditation as a means to fall asleep. There are many different types of sleep mediations out there. But here are three simple ones to get you started:

Body Relaxation Meditation

This meditation practice focuses on relaxing each part of your body. Start by laying in a comfortable position where your spine is nice and straight. Become aware of your breathing pattern without trying to force your breaths. Allow your belly to relax when you breath in and your chest to contract as you exhale. When you are ready, bring your awareness to your feet. Start relaxing your feet by releasing any tension in each area at a time. Release the tension in your toes, the arch of your feet, your heals and then your ankles. Take your time, going at your own pace without rushing. When you are finished with your feet, shift your awareness to your shins and up your legs. Continue up your body until you reach the muscles in your face.

Gratitude Meditation

Enhance relaxation by merging two potent techniques—gratitude and meditation. This meditation is similar to the first technique, but instead of focusing on relaxing each part of your body, focus on sending gratitude. Begin with your feet, thanking them for allowing you to walk and stand. Move your way up your body at your own pace, being as detailed or simple as you like.

Healing Energy Meditation

This meditation practice uses visualization to relax and heal your body. Begin by imagining a calm, warm and healing light engulfing each part of your body. Allow its healing energy to move up your body at your own pace, until your whole body is enveloped in the warm, healing light. Feel the healing and loving energy this light provides.

The Snooze Club: Tips, Tricks & Stress Management

01 REDUCE MORINING STRESSORS

As funny as it may sound, the way you wake up can set the tone for the rest of your day by impacting your mood and energy levels. Alarm clocks that wake you up in a state of stress elevate the stress hormone cortisol and jolt your body out of sleep with a surge of adrenaline. This can have a profound impact on not just your physical body, but your mental wellbeing.

Another common morning stressor that many people overlook is content consumption and social media. Many people start their day by checking their phone, social media or the news. When you begin your day by making your brain process an excess of information and stimuli, it can shock your system into stress. This can actually reduce your energy levels, energy reserve and your focus for the rest of your day.

Reduce stressors in the morning by opting for a less jolting alarm sound and waiting to indulge in social media or other content until you have given yourself time to fully wake up. Instead, create a healthy morning routine that allows you to start your day with more tranquility, peace and allows you to actually enjoy your mornings. This will not only increase your vitality but can have a profound impact on your life as a whole.

02 DON'T HIT SNOOZE

Hitting the snooze button is very tempting, especially when we already feel tired and don't really want to get out of bed. However, hitting the snooze button can actually make you feel even more tired and can become a negative morning habit. You also don't actually get more rest by hitting the snooze button, as the amount of time is often too short to gain any real recuperative benefits. Instead, try to sit up and give yourself some time to walk up.

03 LET THERE BE LIGHT

Your body's internal clock is impacted greatly by light. Light -or the lack there of- influences sleep patterns, mood, apatite and more. Our body's physical, mental and emotional wellbeing are all impacted by our circadian rhythm. Circadian rhythm is our brain's natural regulatory cycle that oversees the changes that happen throughout the course of each day.

The amount of light we give our bodies can have a profound impact on our mood and our energy. Especially if your bedroom is dark in the morning or you have blackout curtains, having a smart light that turns on an hour before you wake up can give you more energy throughout the day and make waking up easier. Opening curtains, spending time in the sun and adding more light to your home or office can increase energy levels, boost mood and add a number of other added health benefits to your life.

04 ADAPTOGENS

We talked about adaptogens under the Can't Sleep Club, but adaptogens can also help rebalance hormone levels, contribute to better sleep, help our body manage stress and increase focus. If you find you are feeling tired throughout the day, your hormones may need rebalanced and your adrenal glands may need a boost. Caffeinated drinks and high cortisol levels can contribute to brain fog, low mood and low energy. Give adaptogens a try and see if you find they help. Side note: It is worth mentioning that some adaptogens can cause fatigue in some people. I recommend taking them at night first to see how your body responds to them before taking them during the day.

05 REDUCE THE CAFFEINE

Don't worry if you just rolled your eyes. Trust me, I love a good cup of coffee in the morning myself. But although caffeine can give you a quick jolt of energy, it also contributes to feelings of anxiety, brain fog, headaches and caffeine crashes that leave us exhausted. All symptoms that may add more disadvantages in the long run in exchange for a quick energy jolt, especially when we are feeling low already. I'm not suggesting you completely give up caffeine. But let's talk a bit about how Caffeine works so you can understand the effects it can have on your body and wellbeing.

Caffeine is a stimulate which means it increases activity in the brain and nervous system. This means caffeine activates the adrenal glans, causing our body to run on adrenaline. Adrenaline increases the stress hormone cortisol in the body. Cortisol increases the glucose levels in the body which is why people who are stressed tend to have a harder time losing weight. In moderation, caffeine can be enjoyable and even have benefits. But when you are consuming it in high doses very single day, your body can become anxious, stressed and fatigued. The National Institute of Health has even linked caffeine to interrupting the release of happy chemicals in the brain, dependency and even withdrawal. Caffeine headaches anyone?

Reducing caffeine or changing the way you ingest it, can have an impact on your wellbeing. Green tea, for instance, is caffeinated just like coffee. However, unlike coffee, green tea generally affects the body more gradually, allowing the energizing effects to last more throughout the day.

Something else to keep in mind is that caffeine can take up to ten hours to clear your bloodstream. This means that you body is still being effected by caffeine long after you are unable to recognize the effects. With that being said, the time you choose to partake in caffeine can have a strong impact on your sleep and feelings of fatigue.

06 EAT WHOLE FOODS

Eating whole foods can give your body the sustenance it needs to make you feel energized throughout the day. Eating foods high in protein can also enhance muscle tone, leave you feeling fuller longer and promote more energy throughout the day. Although sugars and caffeine can offer a spike of energy, it often leads to crashes and higher stress on the body. It's okay to indulge in some sweets or some caffeine, but remember that giving your body the vital nutrients it needs ensures a more sustained and balanced source of energy. It also promotes overall health and well-being as a whole.

07 ENERGY CREATES ENERGY

When we are feeling down it can be difficult to see or even want to see any silver linings, but it is important to remember that energy creates energy. The more negative energies you focus on the more those energies will grow. Whereas, if you focus on the more positive energies then you begin to see more positivity surrounding you. The same can be said of feeling tired and unmotivated. The more you focus on being tired and unmotivated and the more you tell yourself you are tired and unmotivated, the more that energy will stay in your life.

To infuse your life with different energies put your focus on people, activities and things that bring joy, motivation, peace etc. into your life. Shift your energy by doing something that gets you moving even if it's in a small way. Remember you have the power to manipulate energy, but in order for the energy to shift you must choose to shift it. It only takes one small action for the energy to follow suit.

08 GET MOVING

Exercise, even in smaller doses, can increase mood by releasing chemicals in the brain. It doesn't have to be an intensive workout, but get your body moving in a way you enjoy. It can be a simple walk in nature, a bike ride, a hike or whatever sparks your joy. Walking in particular is highly underrated and research suggests it increases problem solving while reducing stress.

09 WHAT IF YOU ARE ACTUALLY JUST TIRED

Sometimes when our body is feeling tired, we don't allow ourselves to truly rest or we think allowing ourselves a bit of extra sleep is somehow unproductive. Sleep is imperative to our bodies and a lot of healing takes place while we are asleep, both in our physical body and our mental/emotional/spiritual body. If you are feeling tired all the time and you haven't been allowing your body more sleep, maybe indulge a bit. Go to bed early. Take

AFFIRMATIONS

Let's start by getting in the right frame of mind.

Here are some affirmations to help you get in the right frame of mind to be honest and productive in this section. Feel free to say these affirmations out loud, write them in the space provided below, adjust them or add to this list. Take what resonates and leave what doesn't.

- This is a safe space.
- It is safe for me to be honest about my relationship and my feelings.
- I am open to seeing the truth(s) of the relationship.
- It is okay to feel my emotions and understand that my emotions may not be an accurate depiction of a situation or contradict it.
- I am on the path to healing.

- **What worked in the relationship?**

- **What didn't work?**

- **List needs that were met in the relationship.**

- **List any needs left unmet in the relationship.**

---

an extra nap. As long as you aren't spending all your time in bed, a little extra sleep can do a world of good.

When you sleep, give yourself permission to sleep. It may sound silly, but saying this out loud or in your head right before sleep can contribute to a better night's sleep or better rest in general.

10 IT'S NOT JUST YOUR BODY

Is your body tired or is your soul tired? There are different types of fatigue, and it's a misconception that fatigue is purely of the physical body. Physical exhaustion may manifest as aches or heaviness in the body, while emotional fatigue can manifest as a weariness towards feeling in general. Spiritual exhaustion may leave a person feeling lost or without purpose, and mental fatigue can be characterized by a diminished capacity to solve problems. Recognizing these distinct types of fatigue is crucial for addressing them effectively. Though they all can take a toll on your physical body, treating only your physical fatigue will not fully heal you. To restore balance, you must work to heal you as a whole.

LOOK TO THE FUTURE

Following a breakup, it's natural to reflect on past memories. However, it's vital to acknowledge that the future holds promise. Your path forward doesn't reside in the past. Redirect your attention towards upcoming opportunities and possibilities. Create a list of things that ignite excitement—a roster of forthcoming ventures, enriching experiences, and meaningful pursuits. Keep this list handy for moments when you require a dose of motivation. Let it serve as a beacon during times of doubt or stagnation. Being single presents an opportune moment to prioritize your desires and needs, while also developing connections with like-minded individuals to enrich your community. Make of list of things to look forward to and that you want to put your energy into.

- ______
- ______
- ______
- ______
- ______
- ______
- ______
- ______
- ______
- ______
- ______
- ______
- ______
- ______

CHAPTER *Eight*

RELATIONSHIP EVALUATION

Looking back on the past can be helpful if we are doing so in a productive way. Reflection is a powerful tool that can help us work through emotions, look at the situation from a more objective standpoint and help us grasp lessons learned so they can be implemented in our journey forward.

The purpose of this section is to provide clarity regarding the overall relationship. It's natural to reminisce about the good aspects of a relationship when we miss someone or feel a void in our lives. However, it is essential to honestly evaluate what genuinely worked and what didn't in the relationship. Honesty within this section will provide you with valuable insights and a more distinct viewpoint on the dynamics and experiences that molded the relationship.

Try to be as honest as you can without casting blame or passing judgement. It is natural for uncomfortable feelings to come up. Take your time in this section and allow yourself to acknowledge the feelings without allowing them to hop in the drivers seat. Remember, aside from your intuition, feelings are not facts and may not be an accurate depiction of what really happened or is happening. Although healing is often accompanied by discomfort, it does not have to be painful or difficult to produce results. Every healing path is unique. You may get better results by allowing your healing journey to flow naturally without trying to force specific feelings or outcomes.

Don't worry if some answers overlap; it can reveal patterns that you might not have been aware of, enhancing your understanding of the relationship's complexities.

- **At what points in the relationship were you happiest?**

- **At what points in the relationship were you the least happy?**

- **What added to the happiness?**

- **What took away from the happiness?**

- **What things could you not share with you partner or not say?**

- **Did you act from any unhealed wounds in the relationship? If so, which ones?**

- **List some things you could have improved on in the relationship.**

- **What fears might you have acted out of during the relationship?**

- **Did you make any justifications for bad behavior on your part during the relationship? If so, what were they?**

- **Why did you use these justifications?**

- **Did you make any justifications for bad behavior on your ex's part during the relationship? If so, what were they?**

- **Why did you use these justifications?**

- **Did you take on any responsibilities that shouldn't have been yours in the relationship? If so, what were they?**

- **If the answer to the above question is yes, why did you take on these responsibilities and what did you think you would gain from doing so?**

- **What was out of your control or not your fault?**

- **Do you feel guilt or shame about anything? If so, list what you feel guilt or shame about and why you feel that way.**

- **List anything you wish you could go back and change.**

- **What can you do to come to terms with what you can not change and accept it?**

- **What boundaries were honored or respected in the relationship?**

- **What boundaries were not honored or respected in the relationship?**

- **How safe did you feel emotionally, physically, mentally and spiritually with your ex?**

- **List any ways your ex was or was not trustworthy.**

- **What were you attracted to in the relationship?**

- **What do you think your ex was attracted to in the relationship?**

- **What did you find attractive about your ex?**

- **What do you think your ex found attractive about you?**

- **In what ways was this attraction fulfilling and what ways was it unfulfilling?**

- **In what ways did your ex express love?**

- **How did your ex show they cared in the relationship?**

- **In what ways did you express love?**

- **How did you show you cared in the relationship?**

- **Were there any ways in which you felt your ex was not thoughtful, considerate or did not express love in a way that was satisfying to you?**

- **In what ways were the expressions of love and care the same and different between you and your ex?**

- **In what ways were the expressions of love and care fulfilling and unfulfilling between you and your ex?**

- **List any ways you felt understood in your relationship?**

- **List any ways you felt misunderstood in your relationship?**

- **What role did you play in the ending of the relationship?**

- **What role did your ex play in ending the relationship?**

- **List the reasons you broke up.**

- **If they broke up with you, write some reminders to yourself that promote self confidence and self worth. An example would be: My ex's choice to leave is not a reflection of my worth.**

- **What was the biggest expectation you had in the relationship that was not met?**

- **Do you feel this expectation is fair and just? If so, in what ways can you ensure this expectation is met in your next relationship?**

- **What does all of this tell you about yourself?**

- **What does all of this tell you about your needs in a relationship?**

CHAPTER *Nine*

THE STEPS OF MANIFESTATION

I want to briefly teach you the fundamentals of manifestation. While this journal mainly aims to guide you through overcoming your past relationships and rediscovering self-love, understanding these steps will give you a deeper understanding of the work we will be focusing on in the next chapter, the key words I will be referencing and the overall process in general. We will be taking a closer look at step two and three in the next chapter, but think of this as laying the foundation in order to move forward.

Manifestation, in a nutshell, has four main steps:
1. **Define What You Want:** First, you need to get very clear on what exactly you want. This is the dream big, nothing is impossible or too crazy to ask for, don't hold anything back step. You want your desires to be big, bold and limitless. Anything that feels impossible will fall into place later on its own. It's not your job to figure out **how** it will all come together. So don't let the fear of the how hold you back. The universe will take care of the how for you. Your job is to define and then align.

I taught you in the gratitude section about root energies. It helps to not only get clear on what you want, but the root energy of what you want. The root energy will help you navigate what energetic transactions you should be prioritizing and what specific energies to be open to receiving. (More on energetic transactions later.) By recognizing the root energy, alignment will be easier and you run less risk of accidentally rejecting your desires due to a lack of recognition.

2. **Release & Redefine:** After your desires have become very clear, you must now remove and release everything in your way to becoming the version of you that has that desire. Sometimes, through the process of decluttering, you will come to the realization that what you want needs to shift, adjust or be redefined. In the next chapter, we will take a deep dive into the many aspects of decluttering, breaking cycles and redefining your desires.

3. **Align:** To attract what you desire you must become the energy and version of you that has that desire. This becoming is the definition of alignment. Alignment is the art of becoming the version of yourself that has your desires by becoming the energy that attracts it. This means you must create new ways of being, feeling, thinking, and doing; create healthy, supportive habits; set intentions; and step into a new version of yourself with consistency. This also means focusing on the experiences you want in your life vs the experiences you don't. It all starts with awareness.

4. **Detach & Be Open To Receiving:** To detach from your desires does not mean you no longer care about them. What it means is you know and believe they are on their way. For that reason, you choose to remain in an energy of faith. This means you don't force or chase after your desires. You also don't wait around for them to come. You do your part in supporting yourself, and then you trust the universe to take care of how it all comes together.

Remember I mentioned that positive energy is like negative energy? It can't influence or enter without your permission because of freewill? This means you have to remain open to receiving your desires and the energies that support your desires in order to have them. In other words, be open to receiving and accepting your good. This also means not accidentally rejecting or preventing your desires from entering your life. For example, if you desire financial freedom, but then get nervous when you have free time because this form of abundance is unfamiliar to you, you could accidentally reject part of the financial freedom you asked for in the first place. It's important to remember that abundance comes in many forms and not all of them are material. Root energies will help you navigate this.

5. **Repeat:** Sometimes there is one more step to the manifestation. You can repeat the process each time you want to manifest something new, or individual steps if you find you are manifesting the wrong energies, outcomes, or experiencing general difficulty with the process. Some manifestations will be easier than others.

DEFINE WHAT YOU WANT

If anything were possible, and nothing and nobody stood in your way, and you could have and be anything you could ever want, what would it be? What do you want? What kind of relationship do you want with yourself? With someone else? Who would you be?

Be as specific as you want. Although we will be mainly focusing on relationships, feel free to write anything that comes to mind. The other things you desire in your life may influence what you want and need in a relationship with yourself and someone else.

If you find you are struggling with this, write down everything you don't want first and then write the opposite of each thing. Knowing who we are and what we want is valuable, but sometimes knowing who are not and what we do not want is just as valuable.

Now that you have written everything you desire, write all the root energies associated with these desires. If you need a refresh course on root energies, go back to the gratitude section of this journal.

CHAPTER *Ten*

CHALLENGING NEGATIVE ENERGY

The first step to creating more positivity and aligning to positivity is awareness. But there's a widespread misunderstanding about how this is done. Many believe it involves identifying and eliminating all negativity. While there's some truth to this notion because awareness supports healing, focusing on negativity doesn't effectively cultivate positivity; it only amplifies it. Positivity flourishes when you concentrate on your vision of it. By diverting your focus and energy away from negativity, its power diminishes.

In other words, rather than engaging in a constant battle to eradicate negativity from your life and the world, choose to invest your time and attention in the positive things you wish to experience or bring to the world. The more you nurture your vision of positivity, the stronger its spiritual energy becomes. Think of it like this: you don't dispel darkness by chasing down shadows with a candle; you dispel it by creating more light. The same principle applies to cultivating positive mindsets and thought patterns.

THINKING POSITIVE

When it comes to creating and maintaining positive mindsets and thought patterns, the same misunderstanding tends to take center stage. Many people believe they must completely eliminate all negative thoughts, fearing that even a single one could disrupt their positive mindset and lead to immediate manifestation of what they don't want.

Let's break down this misconception. What happens when you tell yourself that you can't have any negative thoughts? This directive inadvertently channels your focus towards negativity, generating more negative thoughts. By fixating on the idea of banishing negativity, you inadvertently amplify its presence in your mind. This is the candle chasing the shadows method. While this method may shed light on immediate surroundings through awareness, it fails to banish darkness entirely; it inevitably returns when given the chance.

So how do you create more light in your mind? By channeling your focus and energy into positive thoughts. Rather than attempting to purge negative thoughts, oppose them by replacing them with positive, supportive, or optimistic ones. This is what many spiritual gurus mean when they refer to "selecting your thoughts." And this is also what I mean when I say you must release that which is not yours to make room for what is. Just as you don't control your emotions by suppressing them, you don't shape your mindset by avoiding thoughts.

But won't those negative thoughts manifest what I don't want? The key to manifestation lies in the energy behind it. The reason you manifest what you become instead of what you want is becoming holds the stronger energy. Therefore, one isolated negative thought won't derail your overall progress, mindset, or energetic polarity. Whichever energy there is more of, whether positive or negative, dictates the outcome. Therefore, your mindset is more about the collective energy polarity of your thoughts as a whole rather than individual ones.

POSITIVE RELATIONSHIPS

I've provided examples of how to generate positive energy in your manifestations and mindsets, but how does this translate to people and relationships?

The energy polarity in a relationship hinges on whether there's a predominance of positive or negative energy within it. The challenge arises as each individual brings their unique energetic polarity, shaping their own perception of the relationship's overall polarity. Even if one person exudes a more positive energy, the relationship can still shift into negativity if the other person's negativity overshadows.

So how do you ensure you come to the table with a positive polarity and choose someone else who does the same? The attraction in both romantic and non-romantic relationships starts before you ever even interact with the other person. It starts with you and the energy you are in.

In the upcoming chapter, we will utilize reflection to become more aware of our present energies and identify any negative cycles that might hinder our ability to form more satisfying relationships.

Bear in mind the lessons from this chapter. Instead of aiming to eliminate negative or unwanted energies, consider methods to redirect your focus and attention. The following chapter aims to provide clarity and awareness of your current environment, but it's crucial to remember that awareness alone is just one aspect of the journey towards creating more light.

CHAPTER *Eleven*

CLOSING KARMIC CYCLES & DEBTS

ALL THINGS MUST END BUT NOT ALL ENDINGS ARE EASY

Cycles, seasons and endings are not only natural, they are necessary. Endings and beginnings are the catalysts for change. Yet, recognizing their importance doesn't always make these transitions easier to accept.

IT'S TIME TO BREAK THE CYCLES & FREE YOURSELF FROM INVISIBLE CHAINS

This section was the hardest part of creating this journal. Mainly because this part of the healing process is so incredibly important and unique to each person. Often we are moving forward at such a fast pace from thing to thing that we take little time to slow down, reflect, heal and learn the lessons that will lead us to what we want. This can cause us to get stuck in dissatisfying cycles that leave us broken, unfulfilled, disappointed and jaded, causing us to forget or give up our own power to enact change. In truth, slowing down and reflecting allows us to move forward with more intention. When we act with intention, we become laser focused on the experiences we desire in our lives without allowing ourselves to get side tracked.

Now that you have evaluated your relationship and defined what you desire, I am going to teach you about Karma and how to break toxic cycles so that you can put all your time and energy into the people and experiences you **do** want in your life.

UNDERSTANDING KARMA, KARMIC CYCLES & KARMIC DEBTS

To close out karmic cycles and debts, we must first understand karma itself, karmic debts and karmic cycles as well as some common misconceptions.

Karma is often misunderstood. It is often perceived as a cosmic system that rewards or punishes individuals based on their deeds. This is a common misconception. In reality, karma is a straightforward principle of cause and effect. Our actions and choices serve as the CAUSE, leading to specific positive or negative consequences that have an impact on our lives as the EFFECT. Karma itself is unbiased. We determine its polarity through our intentions and decisions.

People often think karma is here to teach people a lesson. Funny enough, this is actually true, but not in the punishment vs reward way you might think. Karmic lessons are the result of applied understanding of karmic cycles and patterns. These karmic lessons contribute to our spiritual evolution, enlightenment, and awakening. In a negative karmic cycle, they serve as clues to underlying issues, limiting beliefs, default settings, or subconscious barriers and mindsets that could be impacting our everyday existence. In a positive karmic cycle, the lessons are clues as to what to repeat or build upon in order to succeed or level up that area of success.

These lessons are present to foster your self discovery and propel you towards a higher plane of comprehension and self-awareness. It may not seem like it sometimes, but Karma is actually an act of love given to you by the universe to assist you in ascending to the next level of awareness and enlightenment. By teaching you how to improve upon your strengths and turn your perceived weaknesses into assets, you create more resilience, confidence and positive energy towards larger goals in your life. Karma happens for you not to you and the goal of Karma is never to punish, but to enlighten.

Something else to understand about Karma is it pertains to you; your actions, words, thoughts and decisions. For this reason, not everything that happens in your life is a direct result of your Karma. Sometimes we get caught up in the Karma of someone else. Sometimes things happen that are completely out of our control and sometimes we are impacted by the free will of someone else. Although you can not control others or every single thing in your life, you can control how you choose to react to any given situation.

Karmic cycles are recurring patterns in our lives resulting from similar decisions that lead to the same or similar outcomes. A karmic debt arises when the effect of karma comes into play to conclude a specific karmic cycle in someone's life. In a positive karmic cycle, this is the point in which you receive your good. In a negative karmic cycle, when this debt is claimed, a choice is offered: close out the cycle by learning and applying the lesson moving forward, or repeat the cycle until you do.

THERE IS A DIFFERENCE BETWEEN JUSTICE AND REVENGE

Though it may be tempting, it is not your responsibility to administer karma or claim karmic debts; that role belongs to the universe. The universe operates by the law of attraction. By universal law, justice will be served one way or another. Trust that the universe always has your back and is far more creative in administrating its lessons. In my experience, when someone does you wrong the comeuppance always manages to get back to you even if that person is no longer in your life. Still not convinced? Engaging in administering karma or claiming karmic debits can upset the natural balance of the universe and is a misuse of your time, energy and creativity. It might even introduce new negative karmic cycles into your life. Rule of thumb, just don't do it. Focus on you. Put all that energy into bettering your own life. You will benefit more by doing this.

The energy you give out to the universe is the energy you receive back. This is where the idea of energy being amplified by karma comes from. The more good you send out the more you receive back though it may not always return in the exact, identical form.

BREAKING KARMIC CYCLES & CLAIMING KARMIC DEBTS

To break a karmic cycle, you must grasp the lesson associated with it and make different choices that apply the lesson. Failing to learn the lesson and attempting to evade karmic debts will result in the cycle repeating until the lesson is applied not just understood. Breaking a karmic cycle hinges on understanding **and** applying the lesson it holds not just making different choices. Making different choices without understanding the lesson will only bring you slightly different outcomes.

THE LAW OF ATTRACTION

What sometimes perplexes people about karma is the universal Law of Attraction that states "like attracts like and what you give you receive." While this universal principle holds true, karma remains impartial. It's the energy we, as potent manifestors, emit into the world that subsequently gets reflected back to us. Therefore, the energy you emit plays a pivotal role in shaping the energy that returns to you, making you the ultimate determining factor in this process and your relationships mirrors of what is going on with the energy inside you. This also means that whatever energy you are manifesting in, you will receive in the same energy. This is why intention is so important. Acting with intention directs the energies to your desired outcome.

YOU ATTRACT THE ENERGY YOU ARE IN NOT WHAT YOU WANT

Like attracts like doesn't mean that if you like an energy you attract it. It means that whatever energy you are in is the energy you attract to you. I know what you are thinking...

SO WTF?!

This may have you asking questions like, "why do I keep attracting people who are inconsiderate, untrustworthy, unfaithful, unavailable or are the wrong fit? What is wrong with me? WTF?" Let me be the first to tell you there is nothing wrong with you. Attracting the wrong people doesn't mean you are a bad person, the universe is against you, you are being punished or you are unworthy of love. However, it's possible that you haven't yet fully grasped how to align to your desired timeline and how to become the version of you that has your desires.

Let's start with some basics:

YOU ARE ALWAYS COMMUNICATING TO THE UNIVERSE

It sounds simple enough: to break the cycle, learn the lesson; to materialize our desires, become the desired energy. However, at times we become trapped in these cycles because we fail to recognize that we're not communicating as clearly with the universe as we assume. Your manifestation ability isn't like a light switch that you can simply turn on or off; it's continuously active. This implies that your communication must not only be clear but also consistent if you wish to manifest your desires. So, how can you effectively convey to the universe what you truly desire?

UNIVERSAL CURRENCY & ENERGETIC TRANSACTIONS

It's all about energy. In order to come into alignment with what it is we desire to manifest we must first understand the universal currencies are time and energy. Your time and energy are the most valuable things you can give to someone or something because it determines the energetic worth. Who and what you give your time and energy to are what I like to call energetic transactions. The energetic transactions you make tell the universe what it is you prioritize and value. These transactions also are your way of communicating to the universe through the universal language of energy. The greater the number of energetic transactions you invest in someone or something, the more substantial the energetic commitment becomes, and subsequently, the more potent the energy associated with it grows.

In other words, if you have more energetic transactions with people who do not align with your desired experience, you are communicating to the universe that is what you value and prioritize. Your power of creation is going towards people and experiences that match that vibration. On the flip side, if you put your energetic transactions behind aligned people and experiences, you are communicating to the universe that is what you value and prioritize instead. Your energetic transactions are your means to putting in your order to the universe.

WHAT IS ENERGY?

The short answer is everything is energy and everything is made up of energy. But more specifically, as it pertains to alignment, your thoughts, feelings, actions and ways of being are all energy. The more you think, feel, do and be in a consistent pattern, the more that energy grows and the more energetic transactions you give to the value of that way of existing.

To fully become and align to your desired timeline, you must think, feel, do and be the energy and version of you that has and attracts the desire. Sometimes these shifts are subtle and small. Other times, a lot of inner work must be done in order to reshape the world around you. The greater the shift in timelines, the more change is needed to make the shift happen and the more of a different energy you must consistently add into your everyday life.

THE LAW OF FREEWILL

The universal law of freewill means that we are always given a choice. It means that your abundance cannot override your freewill. Your happiness cannot override your freewill. The universe, spirit, God or your spirit guides can not override your free will. Translation? You have to choose your abundance. You have to choose your happiness. You have to ask if you want help or intervention from the universe, spirit, God or your guides. If you want something fixed, you have to choose to fix it. If you want something to change, you have to choose change. It is your choice. You have to choose that which you desire in your life. But it’s not just about choosing. Becoming can also be allowing, receiving, deciding or acting.

This also means that your manifestations and abundance cannot override the freewill of another person. You don't manifest your soulmate by forcing or convincing another person to choose you. You don't manifest your inner circle by compelling other people to join it. Youdon't manifest a new best friend by pressuring someone into being your best friend. It must be a choice freely made by both you and the other person. And, you don't manifest someone becoming the person you want them to be by pretending they are who you want them to be or by falling in love with the idea of them being the person you desire. If you want to "manifest" people, you do it by aligning to the energy you want to attract. You "manifest" a person when your individual decisions align to the same intention and desires of your own volition. Everything begins and is born from within. Like attracts like, but it is always a choice. And it starts with loving yourself the way you want someone else to love you so that you can not only give but recieve the love you desire. To fully align you must become that which you desire first and part of that becoming is doing the inner work first.

STOP WAITING ON GOD

Sometimes, the divine timing you are waiting on is you. Patience and waiting are not the same energy or intention. Waiting is coming from a place of lack. The universe gave you the power of freewill for a reason. You were trusted with the power to decide, to choose and act because the universe acknowledges you are more than capable of taking the self accountability to achieve your dreams and goals. So stop giving your power away by waiting on God to give you the power you had all along. The ruby slippers are already on your feet. Taking accountability for our lives gives us the power to make the changes we need to make in order to release that which is not serving us and make room for that which is.

AS WITHIN SO WITHOUT

Everything in your physical world starts from your inner world. If you want the Law of Attraction to work for you, you must understand how to attract the energy you desire to attract. This is where alignment comes in. It all starts with how you feel and think about the various people, situations and things in your life. But most of all, it starts with how you think and feel about yourself. What we feel and think we become. If you want to create love, happiness and abundance in your outer world, you must first create it in your inner world. You do this by building an authentic relationship with yourself that is not based on outside validation or instant gratification.

Many people think that because they exist they automatically know themselves and have a good relationship with self. However, your relationship to self is like any other relationship. It requires some work, honesty, trust and respect. Self awareness and a good relationship to self is not inherent. It is something you create for yourself and have to maintain.

Don't forget that you are and have always been a divine being. Alignment isn't about becoming worthy or changing yourself in order to be worthy. This can cause you to get addicted to being in a constant state of self help and self improvement. Any changes you choose to make should be because you desire the change and know it's in support of your best interest. You have always been worthy. It's less about changing yourself to attract what you want and it's more about releasing that which is not yours to make room for what is. It's about allowing the best to come through in all situations.

The person who sabotages us the most is often ourselves. Releasing can sometimes be more important than receiving.

TAKING ACCOUNTABILITY. YOU ARE NOT A VICTIM

This serves as a trigger warning, as the following may evoke strong emotions. While it's essential to recognize that mistreatment by others is never acceptable and sometimes things happen outside our control, it's equally crucial to acknowledge our role in choosing to remain in any negative or toxic relationships. Ultimately, no one can continuously mistreat us or make us feel anything without our consent. Enduring negative behavior is a reflection of our self-perception, no matter how inaccurate that perception may be.

Choosing to put up with mistreatment suggests, deep down, a belief that we deserve it. At some point, we allowed ourselves or others to convince us of our diminished worth. We face a choice: perpetuate a victim narrative or embrace accountability, affirming our worth and deserving of better treatment. By embracing accountability and affirming our true worth, we rewrite our past and transform from victim to the hero that survived and overcame.

When we attribute our choices to external factors, we surrender our power. This implies a lack of control, despite the reality that we possess and exercised agency in the situation. While accountability and ownership may be intimidating, they give us the tools, power, and capacity to take charge and institute the necessary changes for a more fulfilling and joyful life. You suddenly begin to realize how much power you have to accept or reject better in your life.

THE IMPORTANCE OF REFLECTION

Devoting time to introspection not only aligns us with our desires, fostering a more mindful and balanced existence, but it also unveils patterns in our lives and provides valuable insights. Breaking free from karmic cycles involves scrutinizing our life, identifying recurring patterns, making beneficial changes, and assimilating the lessons learned. Yet, the true clarity and divine guidance emerge during the stillness that often follows reflection.

While reflection is pivotal in times of seeking change or navigating uncertainty, it stands as a crucial tool for intentional living. It promotes peace and tranquility as well as assists in helping you release heavy or negative emotions. If you haven't already, I strongly encourage you to establish a regular spiritual practice, allowing you to connect with your higher self's guidance, engage in reflection, connect to the divine energy and approach each day with purpose. Many people use regular meditation and journaling to do this, but find the practice and frequency that works for you. Taking time to slow down may feel like it will take you longer to get to where you want to go, but you will be surprised how easy things begin to come together and how little resistance you experience when you move forward with alignent and intention.

ASK AND YOU SHALL RECIEVE

The universe will work to supply whatever is demanded in the energy in which it is demanded. For this reason, be mindful of the questions you ask when going through important spiritual awakenings such as these. The questions you ask set the tone for the answers you receive. Pose empowering questions, and you'll attract empowering answers; ask disempowering questions, and you'll invite disempowering responses. Alignment isn't just about what you do. It's how you think and how you be.

The universe will always respond to the questions you ask it, but the response is tuned to the energetic frequency embedded in the question. If you ask disempowering questions like "why me?" you'll receive an answer, though it might lack the helpful or motivational qualities found in asking empowering questions, such as "how can I better align with a life of fulfillment?"

THE TRICKLE EFFECT

While romantic relationships often bring the most noticeable obstacles to light due to the significant time spent with our partners, it's crucial to acknowledge that challenges in romantic relationships are often mirrored in non-romantic connections, and vice versa. While progressing through this section, you might find that some questions appear less directly applicable. However, patterns are sometimes more discernible in certain aspects of our lives than others, making it easier to identify and address issues in specific areas. Looking at things from various perspectives can lead to huge breaththroughs that can be of huge benefit to you moving forward.

SHADOW WORK

To create alignment you have to not only acknowledge what you want but work on releasing what you don't. This requires a lot of self awareness and understanding. Shadow work is engaging in the practice of uncovering the hidden truth you hide from yourself. It is a practice that allows you to gently observe yourself, your thoughts, feelings and behaviors in order to gain a deeper understanding of self and your subconscious mind.

The journal prompts in this section are designed to help you work through any karmic cycles and karmic debts so that you can take the lessons learned from the relationship and apply them to your life moving forward. They will prompt the shadow work needed to shed light on that which you have been hiding from yourself.

THE LAW OF BALANCE

There is an old saying that opposites attract. This is true but perhaps not in the ways we may assume. The law of balance states that everything exists with its equal opposite. This means that if something exists the opposite also exists to restore balance. The universe naturally seeks equilibrium, and the existence of dualities is an integral aspect of this balance. One side cannot exist without the other, giving purpose to their coexistence. For instance, the contrast between light and dark is essential; without it, the need for distinguishing terms would vanish.

When we lean toward one energy, we tend to attract or seek its complement to restore balance.

However, extremes in energy may lead to overcompensation, drawing us toward the opposite extreme. This oscillation can result in high highs and low lows, creating pendulum-like experiences in our lives. The key lies in the subtle energy shift between complete opposites and complementary energies. Each energy no matter how subtle has its own energy signature that is determined by its true intention. Learning to get clear on the underlying intentions can make a world of difference in your experiences.

If you notice a pattern of attracting individuals with opposing values, it may signal an imbalance that needs healing or an intention that is out of alignment. While being with partners too similar can lead to stagnation or boredom, complete opposition can generate friction that is unsustainable. Excessive differences in energies can turn an initial attraction sour. Instead, seek complementary elements in relationships and strive for internal balance to attract more stable energies into your life.

WHY & INTENTION

Self-healing is achieved through heightened awareness. When we are conscious, we gain the ability to purposefully direct our thoughts, feelings, words, decisions, and actions. This awareness empowers us to initiate the necessary energy shifts, aligning ourselves with the experiences we genuinely desire.

This segment aims to assist you in recognizing patterns and uncovering the underlying **why** behind recurring cycles in your life. It sheds light on how your intentions and energies may contribute to perpetuating these cycles. Some energies, though seemingly subtle, can significantly impact your life. For instance, being in a relationship for the enhancement of happiness differs significantly from being in one because you are reliant on it for your happiness or worthiness.

This work will help you figure out what energies you are currently in so you can determine what energies you want to become.

HOLD UP. WAIT A MINUTE.

The answers you provided in the previous sections may be needed as a reference through the upcoming section, so it’s important you don’t move forward until you feel ready to do so.

This section is designed to guide you in examining patterns, synchronicities, limiting beliefs, and lessons within your relationships. By inspecting these aspects, you can gain clarity on what has been effective, what hasn't, and identify areas that may require attention before embarking on a new relationship. The objective is to uncover the root causes of any pain or disruption you've encountered. Additionally, this process provides insights into your overall desires and needs within relationships.

Take your time moving through this section at your own pace. Some of these questions may be challenging to answer, evoke intense emotions or give new perspectives that require deep contemplation. It's entirely acceptable if profound revelations don't immediately surface, or if you feel hesitant to explore these deeper layers. You may need to move through this section more slowly and allow the revelations and clarity to come in its own time.

Be as honest as you can with yourself in this section. The goal is to work towards feeling deeply satisfied but that will require deep authenticity to which awareness is the first step. Awareness is the light that reveals and heals the darkest part of ourselves. Give yourself grace as you work through this section, aim to be objective and curious. Give your attention to solving the root of any problems instead of focusing on the pain.

Not all of these questions may be relevant to your situation. If certain questions don't bring anything to mind, it may be a good indication of your stance in that specific area. If a question resonates, but you are unsure of the answer that is okay. That question may require more contemplation and there may be additional help in later sections that can help you navigate that question. Complete what resonates with you and disregard what doesn't but try not to avoid any questions solely because they are challenging.

AFFIRMATIONS

Let's start by getting in the right frame of mind.

Here are some affirmations to help you get in the right frame of mind to be honest and productive in this section. Feel free to say these affirmations out loud, write them in the space provided below, adjust them or add to this list. Take what resonates and leave what doesn't.

- This is a safe space free of judgment.
- It is safe for me to be honest about my relationship and my feelings.
- I am open to seeing things differently.
- I welcome positive change(s) into my life.
- I am learning valuable lessons and am breaking cycles.
- I welcome that which is hidden to reveal itself.

PAIN

What I have come to realize is that the majority of negative karmic cycles are perpetuated by pain, the avoidance of pain or the fear of pain.

There is an old saying that time can heal all wounds. However, this saying has never sat right with me because it lacks specificity. I have never experienced, nor have I met anyone who has experienced, healing simply by allowing time to pass. Time, on its own, does not heal much of anything, and there is no restart button that allows you to skip the healing or karmic process. What you fail to recall is compensated for by emotions, and wounded feelings cannot be healed by forgetfulness. For that reason, I have always said that time alone does not heal pain, but alone time does a world of good. This is because alone time allows you to connect with yourself with fewer outside distractions and influences. It enables you to hear the voice of your most loving self more clearly. The problem arises when you carry unhealed pain with you; in isolation and quiet, that pain becomes louder. In truth, this is your body's way of attempting to draw your attention to what needs healing. However, this initial intensity often leads many people to avoid introspection, solitude, or quiet and instead seek loud, dense, and non-stop distractions.

Here's the thing: your unhealed pain and suffering, when left unattended, will fester. It is like a virus. No matter the physical or mental distance you put between you and the experience that infected you, you will continue to feel symptoms as long as you remain unhealed. Your suffering will perpetuate and then inflict suffering onto others as it infects all your most important relationships and facets of your life. What you do or don't do with your pain will impact you in ways you can't even imagine.

Perhaps the most complex aspect of pain is that each experience is relative and intimate. Some find pleasure in pain, others companionship. Some pain teaches valuable lessons while others perpetuate stagnation. The more you experience pain, the more accustomed you become to feeling it. This can work for or against you. It can mean that your resilience allows you to handle more difficult situations with less stress. Or it can mean that the pain eventually becomes so familiar it dulls your awareness to it to the point that it tricks you into believing you are unaffected. This intimacy can trick us with its familiarity into believing that pain is a part of our identity. Especially when our mind or our body react outside our conscious awareness to protect us. We begin to think and feel as though all the emotions and thoughts that go alone with our disappointments and hurts are part of what defines who we are and the world around us. We begin to believe and even seek out the lies our pain tells us. We can even begin to believe that this pain makes us stronger. Unknowingly we begin to feed the pain and like a parasite that goes unnoticed it gorges itself then lays dormant until it needs to gorge again, plaguing our lives with karmic cycles of pain.

So what heals pain if it is not time and does pain truly make you stronger? The answer to healing pain is...well, healing. The problem is that healing does not happen on its own. At the beginning of this journal, I said, "If you want to find the light in the dark you must first open your eyes." Although this sentence can be a double entendre in the literal sense of opening your eyes to see, what I am really referring to here is awareness. Pain, suffering, and negative karmic cycles are all healed through awareness, while love, compassion, and kindness are deepened by it. Awareness enables you to detach yourself from your emotions, thoughts, and experiences, allowing you to be intentional about how and what defines you. Awareness allows you to give the care and attention to the pain that it needs in order for it to begin healing. It is the first step to beginning treatment but it is not enough to complete it. Like how each wound requires its own treatment in order for healing to begin, so does each painful experience.

Strength doesn't arise from the pain itself. If that were the case, no one would be broken by pain, and conditions like depression wouldn't exist. What truly matters is how you handle the pain, suffering, and destruction—how you assign meaning and power to these experiences in your life. Your choice to move forward from these challenges or remain chained by them determines the extent of their impact on you and the world. It's the intention to be resilient through this process that truly makes you stronger. Ultimately, you have the power to define your pain, as long as you don't let your pain define you. Like all things in your life, the power comes from within you.

Treating Pain

While the healing process may involve the reduction or elimination of pain, sometimes a more constructive objective is not eradication but rather transmutation. Certain wounds may take years, or even lifetimes, for the residual ache to dissipate. Some forms of pain extend beyond the physical realm and catalyze transformation on a spiritual level. This is because pain transcends mere experience or sensation; it is an energy. Although energy cannot be destroyed, it can be transformed.

In certain circumstances, acceptance and acknowledgment alone can transmute pain into productive energy. Other times, it may require a deeper exploration to unearth the roots of the pain and understand how to redirect the energy towards a more positive outcome.

Though some healing journeys may necessitate additional steps or external assistance, the steps outlined below for emotional healing are generally applicable and serve as a solid starting point.

4 Steps Of Healing

1. **Awareness:** You cannot fix what you don't recognize as broken, needing improvement, or in need of change. Becoming aware of the problem, situation, emotions, pain, cycles, etc., is the first step towards healing. This stage involves observation, where patterns begin to emerge.
2. **Acceptance:** This stage involves acknowledgement, acceptance, admission, and taking accountability for your part, improvement and also for your healing. It is accepting that which you cannot change. It's when you create space to feel all of the experience without judgment or avoidance, even if the feelings are painful or uncomfortable.
3. **Release:** After allowing emotions to flow through you, it's time to grieve and/or forgive. This is when you find closure from the experience by taking care of any unfinished business and releasing anything that is not serving you.
4. **Transformation**: Once you have come to terms with and reconciled the past, you must commit to a new future. You cannot find your future in your past, and you must release the past before you can find your future. Create a vision of what you desire for your future and focus on making that vision a reality. Find a way to move on and move forward towards a new beginning.

What pain do you still carry with you? In what ways do you still need to heal?

____

____

____

Are there any patterns you are aware of that you have yet to accept, release or transform?

____

____

____

What do you need to let go of or surrender to?

How do your past disappointments, hurts or pains influence your life and relationships?

Anything that comes after the words "I am," whether in thought or spoken aloud, serves as an affirmation to your identity. Alter the way you communicate with yourself and others regarding your pain. Instead of saying "I am," consider using "I feel." By doing so, you create space by distinguishing the emotions or thoughts from your identity in your internal dialogue or verbal expression. Below, learn to cultivate this space by rephrasing common thoughts and feelings you experience regarding your pain with purposeful separation.

OUTSIDE INFLUENCES

Before breaking a Karmic Cycle, it's crucial to explore our beliefs about love and relationships. While it may seem straightforward, working through this initial section of the Closing Karmic Cycle & Debts chapter in this journal can reveal surprising insights. Understanding our beliefs is key to identifying misalignments in our lives and the default settings we have been operating under.

External influences like society, media, movies, books, music, friends, family, religion, spirituality, and past romantic relationships can shape our perceptions of love and relationships. These influences may offer both true and false narratives that could be impacting our beliefs and decisions in our love life.

In this set of initial questions, I encourage you to observe without judgment. Writing down the first things to come to mind will allow you to gain a deeper understanding and awareness of your beliefs, perspectives and defaults you have been operating under. It's okay if, through this process, you recognize certain beliefs that surprise you or don't align with your desired experience. For now, just write what comes to mind until you feel you have nothing else to say. These questions are designed to bring illumination to certain patters, thoughts, beliefs and ways of being so you can gain deeper awareness of yourself. Remember, anything that comes up that you feel is not serving you can be shifted, changed or rearranged. For now, focus only on observing. We will dive into shifting our beliefs later.

EXAMPLES

For questions asking about the inherent truth of a belief, the goal is not so much to completely disprove but to take a new perspective. Sometimes you will find that certain things are true, but remember The Law of Balance states if you find something to be true then that means the opposite must also be true.

Below are some examples to help you with this section and give you some fresh perspectives.

Example 1

BELIEF:
All romantic partners cheat.

IS THIS BELIEF INHERENTLY TRUE OR CAN YOU TAKE A NEW PERSPECTIVE?
No this belief is not inherently true. There are people in the world who do not cheat. You, yourself, may not cheat. Negative experiences or inexperience with healthy relationships may have reinforced this belief.

Example 2

BELIEF:
A romantic partner must fulfill every single need in a relationship.

IS THIS BELIEF INHERENTLY TRUE OR CAN YOU TAKE A NEW PERSPECTIVE?
No this belief is not inherently true. Although some movies and media like to promote this belief, the expectation that your partner must perfectly fulfill every single need in the relationship puts a lot of pressure on the relationship and that person. It sets you up for disappointment. Many people in happy and healthy relationships have discussed how they have their own friend groups or hobbies, find happiness from within and view their partner as someone who adds to their happiness but is not the single reason for their happiness.

Example 3

BELIEF:
Your romantic partner is supposed to complete you.

IS THIS BELIEF INHERENTLY TRUE OR CAN YOU TAKE A NEW PERSPECTIVE?
No this belief is not inherently true. You are beautiful, complete and whole all on your own. Although your romantic partner should add to your happiness and can even compliment you in many ways, they do not complete you. You do not need to be in a relationship to be whole. As a divine being, you are already whole.

Example 4

BELIEF:
Love is all you need

IS THIS BELIEF INHERENTLY TRUE OR CAN YOU TAKE A NEW PERSPECTIVE?
No this belief is not inherently true. You can love someone with all your heart, but still know that without understanding, honesty and mutual respect you may be left dissatisfied. You also can't love someone into becoming the person you need or love them into loving you the way you wish to be loved.

Example 5

BELIEF:
There is one perfect person out there for you.

IS THIS BELIEF INHERENTLY TRUE OR CAN YOU TAKE A NEW PERSPECTIVE?
No this belief is not inherently true. Firstly, nobody is perfect. Second, love is a choice and you have the power of freewill. If there was only one person, there would be no choice to make. Also, what about widows who are happily married again? There are multiple soulmates and different kinds of soulmates for each person.

Now that you have some ideas, lets get started...

List the different kinds and levels of love that come to mind and define each one for yourself. How are they different and the the same? How are they exhibited?

What are some beliefs that you have around love & relationships?

What are some values & priorities you have surrounding love & relationships?

Think back on your life. What movies, tv shows, music, books or other media influenced your perspective on relationships & love? What beliefs did they reinforce?

How do these beliefs still influence you or your relationships?

Are all these beliefs inherently true? If not, how can you take a new perspective on them?

Think back on your life. How has society influenced your perspective on relationships & love? What beliefs did it reinforce?

How do these beliefs still influence you or your relationships?

Are all these beliefs inherently true? If not, how can you take a new perspective on them?

Think back on your life. How has religion or spirituality influenced your perspective on relationships & love? What beliefs did it reinforce?

How do these beliefs still influence you or your relationships?

Are all these beliefs inherently true? If not, how can you take a new perspective on them?

Think back on your life. How has sexuality and gender influenced your perspective on relationships & love? What beliefs did it reinforce?

How do these beliefs still influence you or your relationships?

Are all these beliefs inherently true? If not, how can you take a new perspective on them?

Think back on your relationship with your parents. How does your relationship influence your perspective on relationships & love?

What beliefs around love & relationships did your parent's relationship teach you?

How do these beliefs still influence you or your relationships?

Are all these beliefs inherently true? If not, how can you take a new perspective on them?

Think back on your previous romantic relationships. How did those relationships influence your perspective on relationships & love?

Think back on your current & previous non-romantic relationships. How do those relationships influence your perspective on relationships & love?

Are all these beliefs inherently true? If not, how can you take a new perspective on them?

How have any of these beliefs influenced your romantic & non-romantic relationships in positive ways?

How have any of these beliefs influenced your romantic & non-romantic relationships in negative ways?

LIST THE ROOT ENERGY OF ALL THE POSITIVE AND NEGATIVE INFLUENCES FROM THE PREVIOUS TWO QUESTIONS.

EXAMPLE: MY PREVIOUS RELATIONSHIPS HAVE TAUGHT ME TO BE CAREFUL WHO I TRUST WHICH CAN BE COMING FROM A ROOT ENERGY OF FEAR. I HAVE LEARNED I CAN ASK FOR HELP WHEN I NEED IT CAN BE COMING FROM A ROOT ENERGY OF SUPPORT OR UNCONDITIONAL LOVE.

Positive	Negative

PERCEPTIONS

What we think about ourselves can have a huge impact on our relationship to self and our relationships as a whole. The perceptions of others can influence what we think about ourselves as well as what we think the perceptions of others are about us. Keep in mind that not all perceptions are accurate. Sometimes we show people only what we want them to see or only give them certain aspects of ourselves. Sometimes people project their internal issues on to us. Sometimes perceptions are nothing more than inaccurate or half baked opinions. For example, a friend may think you don't prioritized your friends when in reality you spend limited time with this friend because you have to draw healthy boundaries around their negativity. An ex may mistake your self confidence for arrogance when confidence is trusting in your decision making and arrogance is putting someone else down to feel superior. Your mom may tell you that you are self centered when really they are projecting their codependency on you. Some random person on social media may decide you are stupid because they didn't bother to read your entire post to recognize you were making a joke.

Take a look at the perceptions present in your life and relationships and see if you can get to the truth underneath the opinions, feelings and assumptions.

What are some positive perceptions you have of yourself?

What evidence do you have that support these perceptions?

What are some negative perceptions you have of yourself?

What evidence do you have that support these negative perceptions?

What evidence do you have that disproves or challenges these negative perceptions?

What are some perceptions your ex had of you?

Are these perceptions that were voiced directly to you or is this an assumption on your part?

If these perceptions are an assumption, list any potential insecurities or unhealed wounds that could be influencing this assumption. In short, where does this assumption come from?

If your ex voiced these perceptions directly, what evidence do you have that supports these perceptions?

If your ex voiced these perceptions directly, what evidence do you have that disproves or challenges these perceptions?

What are some perceptions your family and/or friends have of you/your relationship(s)?

Are these perceptions that were voiced directly to you or is this an assumption on your part?

If these perceptions are an assumption, list any potential insecurities or unhealed wounds that could be influencing this assumption. In short, where does this assumption come from?

If these perceptions were voiced, what evidence do you have that supports these perceptions?

If these perceptions were voiced, what evidence do you have that disproves or challenges these perceptions?

List any other perceptions that may be effecting your relationships.

What evidence do you have that support these negative perceptions?

What evidence do you have that disproves or challenges these negative perceptions?

EXTERNAL VALIDATION

Everything begins with self. Many recurring cycles of karma and relationship challenges often originate from the quest for external validation. We seek this validation externally to fill a void that we have neglected to fill within ourselves.

Because we are always in a constant state of manifestation, our outer world becomes a mirror that reveals patterns of energy that are active in our inner world. When we begin observing our external relationships, we can gain important insight as to what is going on with our relationship to self. Humans recognize patterns and we identify with the traits in others that we experience within. This means that any judgments or negativity we hold towards others are typically a manifestation of the judgment or negativity we hold within ourselves. Similarly, any positivity, love, strength or support we see in others is typically a manifestation of the positivity, love, strength and support we have within ourselves.

To break free from karmic cycles rooted in external validation, the initial step involves recognizing where we seek external validation in our relationships. Identifying the areas where we expect relationships to fulfill our needs—whether for love, purpose, importance, comfort, support, attention, etc.—enables us to redirect these needs toward healthier, internal sources.

The tricky part with external validation is that sometimes it likes to masquerade about in disguise. Getting to the root cause sometimes takes a bit of patience. This section will shed some light on some common masquerading validations and validation rooted karmic cycles.

Infidelity

When you hear the word infidelity, many people immediately think of cheating. Although cheating can be a form of infidelity, infidelity is any unfaithfulness to the intimacy created in a relationship. Infidelity is relative and what one person may consider to be infidelity can be different from another. To give an example, there are some people who are very happy in open relationships and don't feel having sexual interactions with other people while being with their partner is a breach of intimacy.Or they may believe sexual interactions with others is within the boundaries of intimacy as long as their partner is also present. Whereas, someone in a completely monogamous relationship would not feel the same sentiment in either situation.

It's not that one way is right and one way is wrong. Both relationships are exhibiting their power to choose their realities in the relationship. The key is to understand what you value and how to support those values through execution of choice. These exercises aim to assist you in assessing whether infidelity was present in your past relationship and, if so, to understand the underlying reasons behind it.

How do you personally define infidelity, and which specific actions do you categorize as acts of infidelity?

Based on what you wrote above, was there infidelity present in your last relationship?

◯ Yes ◯ No

If you answered yes above, how was infidelity present in your latest relationship?

If you answered yes above, who was the partner who committed infidelity?

◯ You ◯ Your Ex ◯ Both

If you committed the infidelity, why? What were your reasons?

What were you looking for outside of the relationship that you were not getting in the relationship?

Are these things you give yourself already on your own? If not, how can you give these things to yourself without relying on a partner to give it to you?

Why did you pursue the infidelity AND your current relationship instead of ending the relationship you were in first?

What does this tell you about yourself, your values, needs, wants and priorities?

If your ex committed the infidelity, was the indiscretion truly an act that was a misalignment of values/boundaries/intimacy in the relationship or is there any possibility you could have been acting out from unhealed wounds or insecurities?

If you answered the above question as a misalignment of values or boundaries, do you feel you clearly communicated your values and boundaries openly and honestly with your partner?

○ Yes ○ No

If your answer to the above question was no, what held you back from communicating your values and boundaries openly?

If your answer was no, how can you better communicate your values and boundaries in the future?

Now that you have answered the above questions, is it that you need to better communicate or is that you need a partner who can honor your boundaries and definition of intimacy?

If you had a revelation from the last question, list any other indications present that you and your ex did not have the same values or that they did not respect your values?

If you answered that you may have been acting our of unhealed wounds and/or insecurities, what were they?

Are you creating boundaries to support your values or to control your partner?

Are these boundaries feeding your insecurities and fear or supporting your healing?

How can you create boundaries that promote/support your healing instead of feeding your fears/insecurities?

How can you work on these insecurities and/or unhealed wounds without negatively effecting your relationships?

List any areas in the relationship you were focusing on the wrong things? Example: physical intimacy instead of emotional intimacy?

What need(s) or desire(s) did this stem from?

What are healthier ways in which you can move forward?

Disappearing Acts & Authenticity (Don't skip this section!)

Although your partner and your relationship should be one of your priorities once you have established a committed relationship, your partner and your relationship should not be your whole purpose and identity. Changing your appearance for your partner, no longer seeing friends and family (Note: This is referring to healthy relationships not toxic or unhealthy relationships you may have removed to promote healthy boundaries) , forgoing your own needs or interests, spending all your time and energy only on your partner, people pleasing, abandoning self identity or abandoning authenticity are all ways in which you may be disappearing into your partner or relationship. This kind of disappearing act is not an authentic representation of who you are or your value. It is not supporting your self care, self acceptance, self love, self worth or self knowledge. (Side note: If your partner made an active attempt to isolate you from other people in your life, this can be a huge red flag for abuse and is not the same thing as you choosing to disappear into the relationship.)

To get to the root energies of this karmic cycle, you must first begin to ask empowering and profound questions.

If I asked you to tell me who you are, what would you say?

Now tell me who you are without including your age, gender, sexuality, religion, occupation, relationship status, how much money you do or don't make, social status or education.

If you felt stumped by that last question, you are not alone. It's a simple question, but incredibly profound and you would be surprised how many people can't answer that question without a great deal of thought.

I ask you this question because I want you to recognize that you are not your age. You are not your gender. You are not your occupation, relationship status, how much money you have. You are not your social status or education level. You are not the labels that society, your friends, family or even you may put on yourself. Your true identity is not found in these labels.

If you're uncertain about how to respond to the last question, that's perfectly fine. I recommend giving yourself some time to allow the answer to naturally emerge. Your response to this question holds significance not only if you tend to disappear into relationships but also in gaining insights into yourself at a fundamental level and understanding your soul's life purpose.

Were you guilty of changing your appearance for your partner, no longer seeing friends and family, forgoing your own needs/interests/hobbies, spending all your time and energy only on your partner, people pleasing, being inauthentic, or abandoning self identity in your latest relationship?

○ Yes ○ No

If you said yes, which disappearing acts were you guilty of?

Why did you engage in these disappearing acts? What did you think you would gain or what were you afraid of?

What can you do differently in your next relationship?

What are some positive changes you notice in yourself when in a relationship?

What are some negative changes you notice in yourself when in a relationship?

Are there any ways you can better cultivate the positive changes?

Are there any ways you prevent or counteract the negative changes?

At what points, if any, were you dishonest with yourself during the latest relationship? If you were dishonest, about what and why?

How can you be more honest with yourself in the future & support an environment of authenticity?

How can you be more authentic or better embrace your authenticity in your next relationship?

What are some ways you can practice self care in general and in future relationships? We will take a deeper look at self care later in this chapter.

How can you better balance your time and energy in future relationships between friends, family, relationship time, hobbies and time for self?

How can you better honor yourself and your needs in general and in future relationships?

What is causing you to want to disappear?

Is there anything about yourself that you wish you could change or you feel isn't good enough?

Were there any needs that you were ignoring or that you abandoned in the relationship?

Why did you ignore or abandon these needs? What did you stand to gain or thought you could lose ?

How can you better communicate and honor these needs in the future?

What can you do to prevent yourself from ignoring or abandoning these needs in the future?

List anything for which you hold blame, guilt, or shame concerning disappearing acts.

How can you accept, heal, forgive and reconcile the above for yourself?

Codependence

Codependence is a type of relationship imbalance where a partner or both partners are reliant on each other emotionally, mentally, physically and/or spiritually. Although it is possible for only one partner to be codependent, this dynamic frequently materializes with one partner assuming the role of the excessively giving caretaker, while the other becomes the overly dependent recipient.

As we covered in the chapter of this journal where we took stock of your support system, there are four main types of support: physical, emotional, mental & spiritual. Although some types of support can include lightening the load of a person's responsibilities temporarily, a lack of balance between giving and receiving can fall into codependency. The difference between support and codependency is the placement of accountability. Support works to offer assistance to solve or heal a problem while providing accountability to those responsible. Codependency enables the problem by taking on the responsibilities of another person for which they should be accountable or holding an expectation of such.

Overly Dependent Recipient

The codependency of an overly dependent recipient tends to be more obvious and easily recognized. Individuals and partners may criticize such recipients for "exploiting generosity" or being "incapable of independent action."

Identifying Some Signs of Excessive Dependence:

Here are some ways in which excessive dependency can manifest. It's essential to recognize that some or all of these symptoms may be evident. Additionally, certain signs can also be present in non-codependent relationships. The tipping point into codependency is often determined by the placement of accountability as well as the degree of excessiveness and frequency. There will also be multiple symptoms present in codependent dynamics.

- Expecting others to be the source of happiness, love, worthiness, or any other external validation.
- Difficulty being alone or doing things alone.
- Struggling with or avoiding independent decision-making.
- Chronic fear of abandonment or rejection.
- Experiencing complete devastation upon the end of a relationship or during conflicts.
- Feelings of helplessness due to doubts surrounding ability and skill.
- Excessive submissiveness or avoidance of conflict at the expense of wellbeing.
- Needing constant reassurance.
- Evading responsibility due to the fear of disappointing a partner or feeling incapable of handling it.
- Possessiveness or jealousy.
- Needing constant attention from your partner whether it is negative or positive attention.
- Relying on or expecting someone else to provide you with purpose in your life.
- Disappearing acts.
- Anxiety.
- The need to control your partner.
- Excessive fixation on your partners every little move, words, actions, interactions or feelings.
- People pleasing.
- Apologizing habitually for things that don't require an apology.

Excessively Giving Caretaker

It may surprise you to find over-giving is a less easily recognized form of codependency. Many people who fall into the over-giving category tend to think they are over-giving because they are loving, generous and kind. Although all three things and more may be true, over-giving is not a pure expression of love nor is it the ultimate act of selflessness. It is often one energy mistaken for another.

Over-giving Masquerades In Disguise

Unlike an excessively dependent individual, excessively giving caretakers tend to receive less criticism from members of their inner circle and sometimes even their partners, as their codependency masquerades under the guise of generosity, love, selflessness, and kindness. This sometimes makes it more difficult to spot. The main difference between true generosity and over-giving is the personal gain. True generosity is giving without the expectation of personal gain or the need to receive something in return. Unconditional love is loving someone as they are without conditions or hoops they must jump through. Kindness is the act of friendliness, generosity and consideration. Selflessness is caring for the needs and wishes of someone else over your own with generosity and kindness.

An excessively giving caretaker engages in giving due to their dependency on the external validation they expect or derive from the act of giving. They give to receive love, respect, a sense of worth, purpose, likability, importance, or some other form of external validation from the person(s) and situation(s) to which they over-give. After extending more than deemed appropriate, they frequently experience feelings of being taken advantage of, unappreciated, depleted, and harbor resentment towards the individuals or situations to which they gave.

To add to the complexity of over giving, intentions and desires can be complex and multifaceted. There are many dynamics in which giving AND wanting to feel good about it is healthy. However, the distinction lies in the subtle energy of need, dependency, and reliance compared to want, support, and gratitude.

Identifying Some Signs of Over-Giving:

Here are some ways in which over giving can manifest. It's essential to recognize that some or all of these symptoms may be evident. Additionally, certain signs can also be present in non-codependent relationships. The tipping point into codependency is often determined by the degree of excessiveness and frequency as well as the presence of multiple symptoms. The placement of accountability is also a main indication.

- Frequently giving or doing more than intended in excess.
- Taking on responsibilities for which others should be accountable.
- Struggling with, refusing or an attitude of cynicism towards help and delegation.
- Giving may flow effortlessly, but there may be challenges in accepting gifts, compliments, or positive gestures.
- Feeling resentment toward giving and blaming others for your lack of time, energy, or money.
- Giving to gain likability, respect, importance, love or another external validation.
- Feeling depleted, unsupported or under appreciated when giving or doing things for others.
- Feeling angry or upset after giving when failing to receive the expected or intended reaction or outcome. Resentment when certain expectations are not met when it comes to reciprocity or receiving.
- Struggling with or never saying no.
- Apologizing habitually for things that don't require an apology.
- Chronic fear of abandonment or rejection.
- Lacking trust and feeling the need to control people, situations, and outcomes.
- Utilizing assistance as a distraction from one's own responsibilities or problems.
- People pleasing.
- Experiencing complete devastation upon the end of a relationship or during conflicts.
- Excessive submissiveness or avoidance of conflict at the expense of wellbeing.
- Needing constant reassurance.
- Possessiveness or jealousy.

- Needing constant attention from your partner whether it is negative or positive attention.
- Relying on or expecting someone else to provide you with purpose in your life.
- Disappearing acts.
- Anxiety.
- Excessive fixation on your partners every little move, words, actions, interactions or feelings.

Codependency is A Disservice To You & Your Partner.

Codependency, whether through over-giving or excessive dependence, results in a disservice to you and your partner. Both forms of codependency foster insecurities in both parties, hinder growth and the breaking of karmic cycles, and perpetuate cycles of unworthiness, low self-confidence, low self-esteem, low self-love, and low self-acceptance.

Regaining Your Freedom From Codependency

Your outer world is a reflection of your inner world. To free yourself from codependent karmic cycles, work to receive the validations you seek externally through your relationships independently from yourself. This is done through self worth, self love, self acceptance, self confidence and self esteem work.

We will dive more into this work later. For now, let's work to gain awareness on any codependency that may be present. Take your time with this section. It may take some patience for the answers or clarity to come to you. If you find yourself getting frustrated, take a break. Professional help may be useful in overcoming codependent karmic cycles as the roots of these unhealed wounds can run deep.

Identify if codepenecy existed in your last relationship. If so, in what ways?

If you were the codependent partner, identify the external validations you were seeking from the relationship? If you find this questions difficult to answer, try identifying what insecurities/fears you were acting from in the relationship instead and it will lead you to clarity.

Why did you seek this external validation? What you did feel you needed or were lacking?

List any areas in your non-romantic relationships that you look for external validation from friends or family.

Why do you seek this external validation? What you do feel you need or are lacking?

How can you give validation you seek from others to yourself or how can you self soothe your insecurities/fears without relying on someone else? What may need to be healed?

If your ex was the codependent partner, in what ways did you perpetuate the cycle of codependence?

If your ex was the codependent partner, in what ways may you have attracted this energy into your life?

What can you do to break this cycle?

In what ways might you have relied on your partner in unhealthy ways?

How can you take accountability and better rely on yourself for this moving forward?

In what ways might you have allowed your partner to rely on you in unhealthy ways?

How can you better hold your partners accountable for their own responsibilities?

In what ways might you allow others to enable codependent or depentent behaviors on your part?

What do you need to do to take accountability and/or feel confident enough to take accountability?

FEAR & S.A.I.F. COPING MECHANISMS

Having courage does not mean you are never afraid. It is the conscious decision to confront and move forward despite being afraid. Fear, often perceived negatively, acts as a dynamic force that can either propel us forward or hinder our progress, depending on how we choose to engage with it.

In favorable circumstances, fear becomes a powerful short-term motivator, propelling us beyond our comfort zones, offering protection or serving as an indicator of our values and priorities. However, when allowed to take a negative hold, fear transforms into a formidable barrier, surpassing other potential obstacles in its ability to impede our advancement.

2 Types of Fears

Before we move forward, lets take a look at the two types of fear.

- Reasonable Fears: Fears that pose an actual danger or threat.
- Unreasonable Fears: Fears that cause a perception of danger or a threat that can create extreme overreactions or the inability to act when needed.

Fear, whether unreasonable or reasonable, has the potential to compel us into making irrational or detrimental decisions as a coping mechanism rather than confronting the source of our fear. Let's take a look at some common S.A.I.F. coping mechanisms that can promote a false sense of security in our relationships.

Settling: The S of S.A.I.F.

When fear takes the reins of our decision-making, it often nudges us towards choices that compromise our aspirations and standards. In the realm of relationships, this can translate into settling for less than we truly deserve. The apprehension of the unknown or the fear of rejection may convince us to accept situations or partnerships that fall short of providing the depth of fulfillment we truly desire.

By succumbing to fear, we may find ourselves content with merely an "okay" scenario instead of actively pursuing what could be deeply satisfying and aligned with our genuine needs. This fear-induced settling not only impacts our immediate experiences but also has broader implications for our long-term well-being and happiness. It prevents us from embracing opportunities that could lead to profound personal growth, meaningful connections, and a more enriching life journey.

Recognizing and addressing these fears becomes crucial in breaking free from the cycle of settling. By confronting our apprehensions, we empower ourselves to make choices based on authenticity, self-worth, and the pursuit of relationships and experiences that genuinely resonate with our deepest aspirations.

Avoidance : The A of S.A.I.F.

Avoidance, as a coping mechanism, compels us to evade uncomfortable truths, addressing problems, and turn a blind eye to illusions, unhealed wounds, toxicity, and warning signs presented through red flags. While this strategy might provide momentary relief from the immediate discomfort, it takes a substantial toll on our personal growth and the establishment of healthier relationships.

The high price we pay for avoidance becomes evident in our diminished capacity to confront issues head-on and actively work towards lasting solutions. The more avoidance is used as a solution, the easier the cycle of avoidance becomes to perpetuate and the harder real solutions become to implement. This evasion not only perpetuates cycles of disappointment but also hinders the development of resilience and problem-solving skills essential for navigating the complexities of life. Confidence diminishes, rendering long-term solutions seemingly unattainable or beyond reach due to a perceived lack of skill or ability for course correction.

Engaging in avoidance not only obstructs our ability to fully embrace and live in the present moment but also fosters the creation of false narratives. These narratives, born out of the fear of facing the truth, set us up for inevitable disappointment when the actualities of life deviate from the expectations we've constructed. The disillusionment that follows further reinforces the cycle of avoidance.

In broader context, this pattern of avoidance contributes to the perpetuation of harmful dynamics that impact our mental and emotional well-being. By sidestepping crucial issues, we inadvertently feed into toxic cycles that hinder our personal growth, strain relationships, and limit our capacity for genuine connection and fulfillment. Breaking free from this avoidance cycle requires a courageous commitment to facing uncomfortable truths, addressing problems directly, and embracing the challenges of the present moment with authenticity and resilience.

But more importantly, it requires us to stop silencing ourselves and stop forcing ourselves to remain passive to that which is not in alignment. Only then can we pave the way for genuine growth, healthier relationships, and a more fulfilling life journey.

Impatience: The I of S.A.I.F.

Impatience, as a manifestation of fear, finds its roots in the anxiety of missing out on opportunities or the fear of not receiving what we desire. This restless urgency can exert a significant impact on our decision-making within relationships, prompting us to settle for less, sidestep potentially enriching experiences, and coerce situations to fit predefined checkboxes.

The pressure to hastily fulfill certain expectations, whether societal or personal, may lead us to overlook the true essence of fulfillment and satisfaction. In the rush to mark off items on our checklist, we risk sacrificing the authenticity and depth that come with aligning our choices with our genuine desires.

This fear-driven impatience can result in settling for situations, people, or experiences that may not contribute to our long-term well-being or bring about a sense of deep satisfaction. This impulsive approach may create a temporary illusion of progress but often falls short in delivering lasting fulfillment.

To address impatience, it becomes crucial to explore the underlying fears and motivations that drive this urgency. It helps to remind ourselves that, although we can delay it through our decisions, we can not miss out on anything that is truly meant for us. What is yours is already yours.

Force: The F of S.A.I.F.

Under the influence of fear, the impulse to manipulate situations and relationships can become compelling, encouraging us to mold them according to our desires. Yet, no matter how much we attempt to shape a situation, its authenticity will ultimately prevail. The pursuit of forcing something to be what it is not demands a substantial amount of energy, and the inherent truth is that inauthenticity is not sustainable.

Attempting to push a situation beyond its natural state involves a constant conflict against its inherent authenticity. This exertion of force requires ongoing effort and vigilance, contributing to an atmosphere of tension and instability. The dichotomy between the desired facade and the underlying reality creates a conflict that, over time, can lead to exhaustion and emotional strain.

Authenticity, on the other hand, thrives in an environment of acceptance and truth. Rather than expending energy on trying to force conformity, embracing the genuine nature of a situation or relationship allows for a more sustainable and harmonious existence. Recognizing and appreciating the inherent authenticity of a situation not only preserves our energy but also fosters a healthier, more resilient foundation for genuine connections and experiences. It is in the acceptance of what truly is, without the need for forceful alterations, that we find a sustainable path toward fulfillment and contentment.

Some Common SAIF Coping Mechanism Manifestations:

- **Check-Listing:** These are "good on paper relationships" that check certain boxes but fail to deeply satisfy or fulfill.
- **Falling For Potential:** Though the appeal of potential is unmistakable, disregarding a significant disparity between potential and tangible realization may result in a repetitive cycle of letdowns. Genuine love is accepting someone for who they truly are as they are. If you only love the potential, you have fallen for an illusion as potential without actualization is not real. People will always show you who they truly are and when they do, it is in your best interest to trust in that authenticity.
- **Love Is All You Need Syndrome:** What about the love you have for yourself and your wellbeing? The idea that love is all you need is a beautiful idea, but love alone will not sustain a healthy relationship. There must also be acceptance, respect, trust and understanding among other things. Real love offers forgiveness, but forgiveness is not the same thing as unlimited tolerance.

You can love someone and know that they are not good for you. If you are practicing unlimited tolerance, you are using S.A.I.F. coping mechanisms to avoid confronting the real problem head on.

- **Avoiding Expiration Dates:** Unfortunately, some relationships have a shelf life and are not meant to stay in your life forever. Engaging in repetitive cycles of breaking up and reconciling, or attempting to coerce a non-functional situation into viability, only serves to prolong the inevitable and intensify the associated pain.
- **Fear of Leaving, Starting Over or Being Alone:** The end of one relationship does not have to mean anything negative about your future. Time invested is not a direct reflection of your progress or connectedness. Enjoying alone time does not mean codependency can't also be present. A lifetime of pain and disappointment is not worth avoiding a temporary discomfort.
- **Toxic Sympathy & Empathy:** Forgiveness and empathy/sympathy are not the same thing. Being empathetic or sympathetic towards the wrong doings of others does not make you are more understanding, less combative or a nicer/more loving person. The justifications and rationalizations of the wrong impress those limitations on you and the person who did the wrong resulting in repeat karmic cycles. When you make justifications and rationalizations for wrong doings, the lines of your boundaries begin to slowly expand until they become unrecognizable. Wrong is wrong. You can not sympathize or empathize someone into loving you the way you should be loved, treating you the way you should be treated or to change their ways.
- **Avoiding Red Flags & Ignoring Intuition:** Doubt is insidious. It has a way of sneaking in and readjusting boundaries to allow for more doubt. Your intuition is a powerful tool and it never lies. Your higher self always knows what is in your best interest and what is not. A good rule of thumb is if it feels like something isn't right then something isn't right. Save yourself the time or energy in investigating why. There are more important matters that will benefit from your time and energy. Learn to listen to your intuition. Whether you do or don't, the truth will be always be shown to you, but when you choose to listen you get faster positive results.
- **Scripting:** Scripting is what I refer to as mentally casting a situation or person into a role to promote a certain illusion and then getting disappointed when that situation or person does not perform the role in the illusion we wrote for them in the first place. This form of toxic optimism distorts our perception of the person or situation to fill a need in our lives. For instance, envisioning someone as our best friend, despite their actions not aligning with that role, can lead to frustration when they fail to meet our expectations of the best friend role.
- **Toxicity, Unhealed Wounds & Insecurities:** Wounds that go untreated have a way of festering. If you do not heal your pain and suffering it will begin to leak out into your other relationships. Handle your wounds. Don't let them handle you.
- **Extreme Independence:** The compulsion to demonstrate our self-sufficiency and competence may hinder our ability to accept support and be emotionally vulnerable. This inclination can lead to neglecting our emotional needs and making choices that foster emotional unavailability, thereby impairing our capacity to form deeper connections.

Consider these questions to reflect on your fears, examining the instances where they may have restrained or propelled you forward to gain insights into the impact of fear on your journey. Reflect on the moments where fear held you back, preventing you from exploring new opportunities or realizing your full potential. Similarly, explore instances where fear acted as a catalyst for positive change, pushing you to overcome challenges and achieve personal growth.

By understanding the nuances of your relationship with fear, you can empower yourself to make conscious choices, turning fear into a constructive force that propels you toward your goals rather than a hindrance that holds you back. Embracing courage involves acknowledging fear's presence and leveraging it as a tool for resilience and personal development.

Write anything that comes to mind from the statements above:

Don't worry if some of these questions in this next section have repeat answers. These questions are designed to give you new perspectives and to reveal hidden patterns. Multiple S.A.I.F. coping mechanisms can also be at play simultaneously.

Avoidance

There are many reasons for why we may choose to ignore, overlook or avoid a problem. Sometimes avoiding conflict may seem like choosing our battles, low self worth may seem like abandonment, intuition may seem like paranoia or manipulation may seem like truth.

In this section, take a moment to identify any issues or problems that were ignored, overlooked or avoided to gain awareness and clarity for our path forward.

Red Flags

WERE THERE ANY RED FLAGS YOU OVERLOOKED, IGNORED OR AVOIDED IN YOUR LATEST RELATIONSHIP?

- ◯ Yes
- ◯ No

If so, what were they?

List anything your ex did or said that was an indication of the red flag(s).

What thoughts or feelings did you have that were an indication of the red flag(s)?

List any patterns or synchronicities that were an indication of the red flag(s).

Why did you overlook, ignore or avoid these red flags, signs and patterns?

What did you stand to gain or lose by ignoring, avoiding or overlooking these red flags?

Did you actually gain or lose any of the above? ◯ **Yes** ◯ **No**

Notes:

Was it worth it? ◯ **Yes** ◯ **No**

Notes:

How can you prevent yourself from ignoring, avoiding or overlooking these red flags in future relationships? What are some signs and patterns you can look for?

WERE THERE ANY RED FLAGS YOU OVERLOOKED, IGNORED OR AVOIDED IN PAST RELATIONSHIP?

◯ **Yes**
◯ **No**

If so, what were they?

List anything your previous exes did or said that was an indication of the red flag(s).

What thoughts or feelings did you have that were an indication of the red flag(s)?

List any patterns or synchronicities that were an indication of the red flag(s).

Why did you overlook, ignore or avoid these red flags, signs and patterns?

What did you stand to gain or lose by ignoring, avoiding or overlooking these red flags?

Did you actually gain or lose any of the above? ◯ **Yes** ◯ **No**

Notes:

Was it worth it? ◯ Yes ◯ No

Notes:

Are there any patterns or synchronicities you can detect between more recent and past relationships in regards to red flags?

How can you prevent yourself from ignoring, avoiding or overlooking these red flags in future relationships? What are some signs and patterns you can look for?

Conflict & Problems

WERE THERE ANY CONFLICTS/PROBLEMS YOU OVERLOOKED, IGNORED OR AVOIDED IN YOUR LATEST RELATIONSHIP? ◯ Yes ◯ No

If so, what were they?

List anything your ex did or said that made the conflict/problems(s) harder to confront.

What thoughts or feelings did you have that made the conflict/problems(s) harder to confront?

List any patterns or synchronicities you detect with the conflict/problem(s).

Why did you overlook, ignore or avoid these conflicts or problems?

What did you stand to gain or lose by ignoring, avoiding or overlooking these conflicts/problems?

Did you actually gain or lose any of the above? ◯ Yes ◯ No

Notes: ______________________________

Was it worth it? ◯ Yes ◯ No

Notes: ______________________________

Are there any patterns or synchronicities you can detect with these conflicts/problems? How do they effect more than just your romantic relationships?

How can you prevent yourself from ignoring, avoiding or overlooking these conflicts/problems in the future?

Toxicity

WAS THERE ANY TOXICITY IN THE RELATIONSHIP?

◯ Yes

◯ No

If so, how was toxicity present? ______________________________

List any ways your ex contributed to the toxicity.

List any ways you contributed to the toxicity.

List any patterns or synchronicities you detect in regard to toxicity.

In what ways did you and your ex perpetuate or reduce the toxicity in the relationship if any?

Did you choose to put up with toxic traits or behaviors? If so, why? What did you stand to gain or lose?

Did you actually gain or lose any of the above? ◯ Yes ◯ No

Notes:

Was it worth it? ◯ Yes ◯ No

Notes:

Does this toxicity effect more than just your romantic relationships? If so, how?

If your answer to the last question was yes, what can you do about it?

What are some ways you can heal any of your toxic traits and prevent them from affecting your present and future relationships?

What are some ways you can recognize and remove toxic traits in your life?

What is the root of these toxic traits? What need or desire do they come from?

If you put up with more than you should have, what boundaries can you put in place to support yourself and how can you better know when it's time to walk away?

Unhealed Wounds & Insecurities

DID YOU ACT OUT OF ANY UNHEALED WOUNDS IN THE RELATIONSHIP?

○ Yes
○ No

If so, what unhealed wounds were present?

How did this effect the relationship?

What is the root of these unhealed wounds? What need or desire do they come from?

What are some ways you can recognize and address these unhealed wounds ?

Do these unhealed wounds effect more than just your romantic relationships? If so, how?

If your answer to the last question was yes, what can you do about it?

List any ways you may be enabling your unhealed wounds to negatively effect you and your relationships.

How can you work towards healing these wounds and prevent them from negatively effecting you/your relationships in the future?

DID YOU ACT OUT OF ANY INSECURITIES IN THE RELATIONSHIP?

- ◯ Yes
- ◯ No

If so, what insecurities were present?

How did this effect the relationship?

What is the root of these insecurities? What need or desire do they come from?

What are some ways you can recognize and address these insecurities?

Do these insecurities effect more than just your romantic relationships? If so, how?

If your answer to the above question was yes, what can you do about it?

List any ways you may be enabling your insecurities to negatively effect you and your relationships.

Illusions

WERE THERE ANY ILLUSIONS AT PLAY IN THE RELATIONSHIP?

- ○ Yes
- ○ No

If so, what illusions were present?

How did you contribute the the illusion(s)?

How did your ex contribute to the illusion(s)?

List anything your ex did or said that was an indication of the illusion(s).

What thoughts or feelings did you have that were an indication of the illusion(s)?

List any patterns or synchronicities that were an indication of the illusion(s).

In what ways did you buy in to the illusion(s)?

Why did you choose to buy into the illusion(s)? What did you stand to gain or lose?

Did you actually gain or lose any of the above? ◯ Yes ◯ No

Notes:

Was it worth it? ◯ Yes ◯ No

Notes:

What is the root of these illusions? What need or desire do they come from?

List any ways you may be enabling illusions to negatively effect you and your relationships.

How can you prevent yourself from ignoring, avoiding or overlooking these illusions in future relationships? What are some signs and patterns you can look for?

Intuition

DID YOU IGNORE YOUR INTUTION DURING THE RELATIONSHIP?

- Yes
- No

If you answered yes above, what specific moments can you recall?

What ways did your intuition try to communicate with you that something was wrong or off?

Why did you ignore your intuition? What added to the doubt?

Are there any specific signals you have noticed from your intuition that indicate yes, no or a neutral response?

How can you better connect to and listen to your intuition moving foward?

Impatience, Forcing & Settling

There are many reasons for why we may grow impatient in our relationship manifestations. Outside pressure placed upon us or internal pressures we place on ourselves can cause impulsive instead of intentional decision making causing us to force situations and/or settle for less.

In this section, take a moment to identify if impatience was present in your decision making and during your relationship.

DID IMPATIENCE PLAY A ROLE IN YOUR DECISION MAKING IN YOUR RELATIONSHIP?

○ **Yes**

○ **No**

If so, in what ways?

DID YOU ATTEMPT TO FORCE AND/OR MANIPULATE ANY SITUATIONS IN YOUR RELATIONSHIP THAT WERE NOT WORKING INTO WORKING?

○ Yes

○ No

If so, what did you try to force or manipulate to work?

DID YOU SETTLE FOR LESS IN ANY WAY IN YOUR RELATIONSHIP?

○ Yes

○ No

If so, in what ways?

What caused you to grow impatient, force situations and/or settle? What did you stand to gain or lose?

Did you actually gain or lose any of the above? ○ Yes ○ No

Notes:

Was it worth it? ◯ **Yes** ◯ **No**

Notes:

What is the root of the impatience, forcing and/or settling? What need or desire does it come from?

How can you make different choices moving forward?

How can you honor your needs and desires in heathier ways?

If you were acting from impatience, how can redefine progress so that it is working for you instead of against you?

An Overview of Fear

Now that we have taken a look at some unhealthy coping mechanisms for fear, let's take a look at how fear may be present or may influence your relationships as a whole.

What are you afraid of?

Are these fears realistic or unrealistic fears?

How has fear influenced your relationship(s)?

What do your fears tell you about your priorities and values?

How can you tackle these fears in healthy ways head on?

How can you harness your fear to work to your advantage?

What are some areas you can work on so fear doesn't get the best of you?

THE INTERNAL SELF

I've said it several times throughout this journal and I am going to say it again because this fact is so important. Everything starts with self. You may not have realized it, but my saying this has been a huge clue as to what the root of all your happiness and sorrow in your relationship stems from. Your inner self and your relationship with your inner self is the foundation in which you build your relationships with others and build your external world.

Now that you have taken a deep dive into your outer influences, perceptions, fears and unmet desires I hope you have begun to see a pattern here. Your relationship experiences come from either a lack or abundance of self confidence, self worth, self acceptance, self esteem or self love. Let's take a deep dive into the internal self and where we can reclaim our power by shifting our attention inward.

Self Confidence:

If I were to ask you what self confidence is you would likely say something like it is feeling good about yourself. Although this isn't exactly a wrong answer, it fails to identify the true depth of where the "good feeling" comes from. What distinguishes true self confidence apart from ego or arrogance is the placement of validation. Ego fosters a deceptive sense of confidence to project an appearance of self-assurance, while holding a belief of unworthiness. Arrogance involves putting others down to elevate oneself. Both rely on external validation to bolster confidence. In contrast, authentic self-confidence emerges from trust and belief in your own abilities and decision-making.

Let's take a look at where your relationships may be influencing your self confidence and where your self confidence may be influencing your relationships.

How confident did you feel prior, during and after your last relationship?

What contributed to your confidence or lack of confidence?

How did your confidence or lack of confidence effect your last relationship?

How does your confidence or lack of confidence effect your non-romantic relationships?

What about this last relationship specifically affected your self confidence positively and negatively?

If your most recent relationship has had an adverse impact on your self confidence, what steps can you take to reconstruct and strengthen your self confidence?

List any ways in which you were relying on your partner or your relationship to make you feel confident.

List any ways in which you allowed your partner or relationship to affect your self confidence in ways you shouldn't have.

How can you remove the need for external validation where it comes to your self confidence?

What can you do to feel more confident in your relationships? What steps can you take? How can you better support and trust yourself in and outside of a relationship?

Is there anything you need to forgive yourself for?

Intuitive Self Confidence:

Intuitive self-confidence refers to the trust and belief you have in your own intuition and intuitive guidance.

How often do you listen to your intuition? What attributes to your decision to listen or not listen?

List a time your intuition spoke to you and you trusted your intuition.

Why did you trust your intuition in this instance? What reasons did you have?

List a time your intuition spoke to you and you did not heed your intuition.

Why didn't you trust your intuition in this instance? What reasons did you have?

Were these good reason? Were these reason good reasons to doubt yourself?

What was the result of the time you listened to your intuition?

What was the result of the time you did not listen to your intuition?

Has your intuition ever been truly wrong in the past? If not, what prevents you from listening to it? If you think it has been wrong, how sure are you it was your intuition speaking?

Self Worth:

Self worth is the valuation you place on yourself, your capabilities and worthiness to receive good. Let's take a look at how self worth affected your relationship and how your relationship affected your self worth.

How worthy did you feel prior, during and after your last relationship?

What contributed to your feelings of worthiness or lack of worthiness?

How did your feelings of worthiness or lack of worthiness effect your last relationship?

How does your sense of worthiness or feelings of unworthiness impact your non-romantic relationships?

What about this last relationship specifically affected your self worth positively or negatively?

If your most recent relationship has had an adverse impact on your self-worth, what steps can you take to reconstruct and strengthen your sense of self-worth?

List any ways in which you were relying on your partner or your relationship to make you feel worthy.

How can you remove the need for external validation where it comes to your self worth?

What can you do to feel more worthy in your relationships? What steps can you take? How can you better support and honor yourself?

Is there anything you need to forgive yourself for?

Self Acceptance:

Self acceptance is the ability to accept both your strengths and perceived weaknesses as part of your authentic being without judgement. It is accepting all aspects of your authentic self. Let's take a look at how self acceptance has influenced your relationships and how your relationships have influenced your self acceptance.

Do you feel you are able to accept yourself as you are? Why or why not?

Did you feel you were accepted in your last relationship for who you are? Why or why not?

How did your sense of acceptance and self acceptance impact your last relationship?

How does your sense of acceptance and self acceptance impact your non-romantic relationships?

What affects your sense of acceptance and self acceptance positively and negatively in general?

What effected your sense of acceptance and self acceptance positively and negatively specifically in your last relationship?

If your most recent relationship has had an adverse impact on your self acceptance, what steps can you take to reconstruct and strengthen your sense of self acceptance?

List any ways in which you were relying on your partner or your relationship to make you feel acceptable.

How can you remove the need for external validation where it comes to your self acceptance?

What can you do to better honor yourself in your relationships? What steps can you take? How can you better support and accept who you really are?

Is there anything you need to forgive yourself for?

Self Love

Self love is how you show, express and hold love and appreciation for yourself. Let's take a look at how self love has impacted your relationships and how your relationships have impacted your self love.

Do you feel that you love yourself for who you really are? Why or why not?

Were you able to maintain and express self love in your last relationship? Why or why not?

How did your sense of self love impact your latest relationship?

How does your sense of self love impact your non-romantic relationships?

What about this latest relationship effected your self love positively and negatively?

What affects your self love positively and negatively in general?

If your most recent relationship has had an adverse impact on your self love, what steps can you take to reconstruct and strengthen your sense of self love?

List any ways in which you were relying on your partner or your relationship to make you feel loved.

How can you remove the need for external validation where it comes to your self love?

What can do to better love yourself in your relationships? What steps can you take? How can you better support and love who you really are in and outside a relationship?

In what ways did you show yourself love and appreciation during your last relationship? In general?

In what ways could you have loved and appreciated yourself better?

Is there anything you need to forgive yourself for?

Self Esteem

Self esteem is the beliefs, thoughts and feelings we hold about ourselves. When self esteem is high we hold more positive beliefs, thoughts and feelings about ourselves. When self esteem is low we hold more negative beliefs, thoughts and feelings about ourselves. Self confidence, self acceptance, self worth and self love all contribute to our self esteem.

Let's take a look at self esteem, how it impacted your relationship and how your relationship impacted your self esteem.

In general, would you say you generally have a high or low self esteem? Why?

How did you feel about yourself during your relationship? Was your experience more postive or negative?

How did your sense of self esteem impact your last relationship?

How does your sense of self esteem impact your non-romantic relationships?

What positively and negatively contributes to your overall self esteem?

What about this latest relationship affected your self esteem positively or negatively?

If your most recent relationship has had an adverse impact on your self esteem, what steps can you take to reconstruct and strengthen your sense of self esteem?

List any ways in which you were relying on your partner or your relationship to boost your self esteem.

How can you remove the need for external validation where it comes to your self esteem?

How can you prevent your relationships from negatively affecting your self esteem?

What can you do to increase the amount of positive thoughts and feelings you have towards yourself?

What can you do to boost your self esteem without the need for external validation? What steps can you take? How can you support the best version of yourself in and outside of a relationship?

In what ways, if any, did you abandon yourself in your latest relationship?

What can you do to better support yourself and create a stronger foundation for yourself in the future?

Is there anything you need to forgive yourself for?

After reflecting on your inner self, what patterns do you notice? What was revealed to you?

What patterns do you notice about your inner self when it comes to relationships?

What areas of your inner self foundation need some work?

What can you do to better support and reinforce the foundation of your inner self?

What can you do for yourself in order to fully accept, love and trust in yourself?

How can you reinforce a positive inner self image for yourself?

How can you create a solid foundation for your inner self no matter what happens?

LIMITING BELIEFS & DEFAULT SETTINGS

Now that you have a deeper understanding of the inner and outer influences that are impacting your inner self, let's build onto what we have learned. The internal and external influences we give our attention shape the foundation of the inner self and our core. We begin to think, feel and be in patterns that support that foundation.

When the foundation is not in alignment with the experiences we wish to experience, this is when we must take a deeper look at how our inner self is operating and the foundation those operations are supporting.

Default Settings:

Default settings are the automatic and reoccurring habits that have become our default way of thinking, feeling, doing and being based on the foundation of our inner self. These defaults can work for us by reinforcing positive patterns or against us by reinforcing negative patterns.

Although our default thoughts, feelings and actions can be very familiar and even feel or sound like us, default settings are not who you are. They are simply the programing you have trained yourself into operating under consciously or subconsciously.

Limiting Beliefs:

Limiting beliefs are beliefs, opinions or states of mind that are based in restriction. They are often the lies we choose to buy into that prevent us from reaching our highest potential or believing in unlimited possibility. Limiting beliefs often contribute to negative default settings that prevent us from aligning to more elevated or enlightened experiences.

Identifying Default Settings & Limited Beliefs

The first step to shifting default settings and limiting beliefs is to identify them. In order to identify default settings and limiting beliefs you must observe the automatic and repeat thoughts, feelings, actions and patterns in your life.

Use the answers you wrote in previous sections to identify any reoccurring thought, feeling or behavior patterns.

List any reoccurring or automatic thoughts you notice surrounding relationships, love and your inner self.

List any reoccurring or automatic feelings you notice surrounding relationships, love and your inner self.

List any reoccurring or automatic actions you notice surrounding relationships, love and your inner self.

List any reoccurring or automatic ways of being you notice surrounding relationships, love and your inner self.

List any reoccurring or automatic patterns you notice in this latest relationship.

List any reoccurring or automatic patterns you notice between this relationship and past relationships.

List any reoccurring or automatic patterns you notice in your non-romantic relationships.

List any reoccurring or automatic patterns you notice between your romantic and non-romantic relationships.

Were there any ways in which you were reacting instead of making intentional decisions in your last relationship?

What about in your life in general?

What stories, lies or beliefs did you tell yourself, did you choose to believe or did these patterns support?

Are any of these patterns or beliefs serving you? Are they a match for what you wish to experience? If not, what are the default settings, limiting beliefs or habits you now recognize you have been operating under and how do they need to shift?

ATTACHMENTS

To break free from negative, toxic or misaligned habits and cycles in order to transition into better, the first crucial step is uncovering the attachments formed to these detrimental patterns. Attachments - not to be confused with attachment styles- are the emotional, physical, spiritual, or mental fulfillment we derive from an experience that attribute to why we perpetuate them.

While attachments are not inherently negative, they lead to dissatisfaction when they manifest in ways misaligned with our authentic or highest self, often resulting in feelings of disappointment, anger, insecurity, or low self-esteem. In extreme cases, these attachments create energy imbalances and even physical symptoms similar to addiction, causing reliance on the high highs that low lows create. The stronger and more complex the attachment, the deeper we must look at our inner self to release or redirect the associated energy.

Let's take a look at some different types of attachments:

4 TYPES OF ATTCHMENTS

Emotional Attachments	Emotional attachments are the emotional gratifications we receive from an experience such as pride after completing a major milestone or the false sense of happiness alcoholics can feel after indulging in drinking.

Mental Attachments	Mental attachment is the validation we seek to reinforce beliefs and thoughts about an experience. It employs logic, practicality & reasoning to either support or challenge patterns in our lives. For instance, repeatedly encountering dishonest partners, may develop mental attachments affirming the belief that all partners are untrustworthy. Whereas, positive affirmations can create positive mental attachments pertaining to self esteem.

Physical Attachments	Physical attachment is the material or bodily sensation derived from a situation. We can create physical attachments to unfulfilling jobs that pay a lot of money or to healthy foods that make us physically energized.
Spiritual Attachments	Spiritual attachment involves emotional, physical, and mental gratifications or reinforcements linked specifically to spiritual, energetic, or religious experiences and practices. It extends to our sense of purpose, existence, spiritual self, identity, soul, and energetic connections. I distinguish this attachment because it assigns extra significance to experiences that might lack such meaning otherwise. For instance, I hold a spiritual attachment to hummingbirds because their unexpected appearance coincides with increased financial abundance in my life. Therefore, hummingbirds have become a spiritual signpost emotionally, mentally and physically in my life pertaining to financial abundance. Whereas to someone else, a hummingbird may simply be a bird.

Attachments are complex and are not mutually exclusive. It might be hard to believe that when you find yourself stuck in a negative habit or cycle, there's some form of emotional gratification and/or reinforcement you are deriving from it even when it is out of alignment with your desires. But after identifying the misaligned habits, beliefs and default settings, identifying what is gained from these patterns, even if the gain could be better manifested, is the next step in exploring how to release or redirect that energy in a healthier, more positive and aligned manner.

Example:

All of us know that one person who is always late and can never be on time to anything. Guess what? In my early twenties, I used to be that person. From the outside looking in, it may be easy to think the fix is as simple as working on time management skills. For some people, this is the case, but for others it could also be a deeper attachment issue causing the karmic wheel to continue down the late-person- who-is-never-on-time-for-anything path. What happens when time management skills alone don't solve this issue?

As a recovered lateoholic, I can personally vouch for those of you who have this problem and have been unable to solve it through simple time management skills. Regardless of how you relate, the late one or the one always waiting for the late one, listen up. I am about to teach you the first lesson in attachments and show you how something like time management can be only a small piece or even irrelevant piece of a much bigger problem.

The reason I use being late as an example is not only because it is highly relatable but because is a great example of how some attachments hide behind deeper rooted unhealed wounds and how attachments are relative to each individual.

In the first example, I will show you how being late can have a simple attachment with an easy fix. I will provide some examples of attachments to give you an idea of how different attachments can come into play. Then I will show you how the same karmic cycle can have a complex attachment by using my own experience as an example.

Example 1: Being Late With Simple Attachments

Identify the negative habit or cycle.

Always being late.

Identify any emotional attachments present. This is any emotional gratification the habit or cycle gives you.

Excitement.

Identify any physical attachments present. This is any material gain or bodily sensation the habit or cycle gives you.

Adrenaline rush.

Identify any mental attachments present. This is any reinforcement of beliefs or thoughts pertaining to the habit or cycle.

My life lacks excitement. I am bad at time management. The expected is boring.

Identify any spiritual attachments present. This is any emotional, physical or mental gratification or/or reinforcement pertaining to spiritual, energetic or religious experiences or practices. It extends to our sense of purpose, existence, spiritual self, identity, soul, and energetic connections.

Not applicable.

If any of the above two answers include limiting beliefs or default settings, how can you challenge these beliefs or defaults?

I can create more healthy excitement in my life. I only think I am bad at time management because that is what others have told me is the problem. Consistency doesn't have to be boring.

What is the root need or desire? How can you remove, redirect, heal or shift this energy to fit with your desired experience?

The person in this example is looking for more adventure and excitement in their life. A solution would be to find a healthier way to fulfill this need. Instead of using being late as the source, maybe go somewhere new or try something new more regularly. Find healthy ways to be spontaneous.

Now that I have given you an example of a more simple attachment to a negative karmic cycle. Let's take a look at the same problem with complex attachments.

For me, when I first took a look at the attachments for why I was always late, my responses looked something like this.(Note: The next two examples are not word-for-word accounts but are rather written in a way that promotes the overall experience and feeling of what happened.):

Example 2: Being Late With Complex Attachments

Identify the negative habit or cycle.

Always being late.

Identify any emotional attachments present. This is any emotional gratification the habit or cycle gives you.

Excitement. Validation for my mental attachments.

Identify any physical attachments present. This is any material gain or bodily sensation the habit or cycle gives you.

Adrenaline rush. Stress that feels familiar and because of that, it feels safe.

Identify any mental attachments present. This is any reinforcement of beliefs or thoughts pertaining to the habit or cycle.

My life lacks excitement. I just suck at time management. Successful people are always busy. There is never enough time in a day. Being busy is normal. Stress is normal. Peace is not safe.

Identify any spiritual attachments present. This is any emotional, physical or mental gratification or/or reinforcement pertaining to spiritual, energetic or religious experiences or practices. It extends to our sense of purpose, existence, spiritual self, identity, soul, and energetic connections.

Not applicable.

If any of the above two answers include limiting beliefs or default settings, how can you challenge these beliefs or defaults?

I can infuse my life with healthy excitement. I meet deadlines on time or early. This is proof I am not actually bad at time management. Success is relative and how hard you work is not the measuring stick for success. It's not that there isn't enough time in a day it's that I have been distracted by tasks that do little to move my progress and I have been disorganized with my goals. Being busy is normal to me but maybe I am more busy then is healthy? Maybe this is why stress feels safe and familiar. I don't know how to relax. Relaxing gives me stress.

What is the root need or desire? How can you remove, redirect, heal or shift this energy to fit with your desired experience?

I guess in terms of the excitement part I can redirect that energy in a healthier way. I guess I can try to leave earlier? AGAIN. I guess I can prioritize tasks in terms of time management?

While I wrote out the above, I felt very proud of myself. My thought pattern went something like this. Feel free to laugh or just feel extremely perplexed. I did and felt both: *Damn. That's good. I figured it out. I am so right. I am just bad with time management and there's never enough time in a day and...wait. Oof. Did I really just think that? Do I really believe that? I always meet my deadlines on time or early. That isn't bad time management. So then why am I always late to go to places? OMG! Am I actually* ***proud*** *that I run late? I am. I shouldn't be. But I am! Ew! I can't believe I just admitted that. Wait. If I am proud of myself for this...why?! Why do situations with less stress give me more stress instead? And how can I shift all of this?*

After this deep revelation, I realized I needed to get out my journal and free write. I share this with you, because I want you to realize just as I did, that this is a process and it's a skill that through some practice you get better and better at. You may not get to the deepest root attachment the first try and that is okay. Sometimes it takes a couple revelations before you get to the deepest attachment and find a long term sustainable solution to the karmic cycle. Be gentle with yourself and try to be patient. Like a lotus flower that opens petal by petal, you get to deeper and deeper layers of yourself by opening up one step at a time.

By taking a deeper dive into the inner self, getting very honest and observing thought, emotion and action patters, you can start recognizing the deeper issues at hand. The thing is, attachments can be sneaky. They can sometimes be hard to pinpoint, hide under more surface level problems or we can be swayed by others to think the problem is something it's not. Case in point, time management. They can also end up being a part of deeper unhealed wounds we have long hidden in the darkest parts of ourselves.

Once I took a long hard look at the first revelation and did some journaling, I realized the real root of this karmic cycle was much deeper than I imagined. The real problem had nothing to do with time management or boredom at all and everything to do with limiting beliefs and default settings I had around success, self worth and progress. I was also going to some events out of obligation to avoid conflict instead of just not going. The next level of attachment analysis looked something like this:

Example 3: Being Late With Complex Attachments Deep Dive

Identify the negative habit or cycle.

Always being late.

Identify any emotional attachments present. This is any emotional gratification the habit or cycle gives you.

I seem to be taking pride in being late because it validates my need to appear successful to others.

Identify any physical attachments present. This is any material gain or bodily sensation the habit or cycle gives you.

N/A

Identify any mental attachments present. This is any reinforcement of beliefs or thoughts pertaining to the habit or cycle.

I do not appear successful. I am not where I want to be in my journey. I am unworthy. People do not respect me. I have nothing to show for the amount of work I put into my life. Why bother showing up at all? If I don't go to these events, even if I truly don't want to go, I will look bad or people will be disappointed in me.

Identify any spiritual attachments present. This is any emotional, physical or mental gratification or/or reinforcement pertaining to spiritual, energetic or religious experiences or practices. It extends to our sense of purpose, existence, spiritual self, identity, soul, and energetic connections.

I have a deep knowing I am supposed to do something important with my life, but somehow I seem to always fall short of my potential and I can't live up to my purpose. What is my purpose anyways? How am I suppose to be who I am supposed to be if I can't figure out how to be successful?

If any of the above two answers include limiting beliefs or default settings, how can you challenge these beliefs or defaults?

Success is relative. I already figured that out in the last analysis. But what is success truly if it is relative? Maybe I need to be asking myself what my definition of success is. I can't be my version of successful if I don't even know how to define it. I am not unworthy, but I feel unworthy. I need to get clear on why I feel that way. I am running out of space. Back to journaling I go...

What is the root need or desire? How can you remove, redirect, heal or shift this energy to fit with your desired experience?

Worthiness, confidence & success. I need to define success for myself and then become that version of myself. I also need to figure out how to feel successful on my own without the need for external validation. I am tying my self identity and my self worth to my perceived success. How can I separate this? I need to work on my self esteem.

As you can see in these examples, the simple karmic cycle of being late ended up having deep seated root attachments in my own life. This was something simple that was effecting me at a fundamental level. These were unhealed wounds, limiting beliefs, a lack of healthy boundaries, avoidance of conflict and default settings I was perpetuating and even taking pride in perpetuating because they validated the negative beliefs I held about myself. This is also why adjusting time management was neither the problem or the solution to this karmic cycle.

IDENTIFYING ATTACHMENTS

Now that you have explored outside influences, perceptions, external validations, fears, coping mechanisms, your internal self, limiting beliefs and default settings that have been attributing to the negative or misaligned karmic cycles in your life, let's identify and remove some negative attachments. Use the answers from previous sections to complete this one.

Identify the negative habit or cycle you wish to break.

How does this cycle or habit make you feel?
List all the emotions, positive and negative.

What thoughts do you notice that pertain to this cycle or habit?

What actions and/or ways of being are part of this cycle or habit?

Identify any emotional attachments present.
This is any emotional gratification the habit or cycle gives you.

Identify any physical attachments present.
This is any material gain or bodily sensation the habit or cycle gives you.

Identify any mental attachments present.
This is any reinforcement of beliefs or thoughts pertaining to the habit or cycle.

Identify any spiritual attachments present.
This is any emotional, physical or mental gratification or/or reinforcement pertaining to spiritual, energetic or religious experiences or practices. It extends to our sense of purpose, existence, spiritual self, identity, soul, and energetic connections.

Challenge the default settings, limiting beliefs and/or negative habits.
If any of the above two answers include limiting beliefs or default settings, how can you challenge these beliefs or defaults? What more positive habits can be substituted?

Identify the root need(s) and/or desire(s).

How can you remove, redirect, heal or shift this energy to fit with your desired experience? Write out new ways of being, thinking, feeling and doing that better serves you.

Use this space to free write. Let your thoughts flow freely until you feel you have nothing else to say or write.

Identify the negative habit or cycle you wish to break.

How does this cycle or habit make you feel?
List all the emotions, positive and negative.

What thoughts do you notice that pertain to this cycle or habit?

What actions and/or ways of being are part of this cycle or habit?

Identify any emotional attachments present.
This is any emotional gratification the habit or cycle gives you.

Identify any physical attachments present.
This is any material gain or bodily sensation the habit or cycle gives you.

Identify any mental attachments present.
This is any reinforcement of beliefs or thoughts pertaining to the habit or cycle.

Identify any spiritual attachments present.
This is any emotional, physical or mental gratification or/or reinforcement pertaining to spiritual, energetic or religious experiences or practices. It extends to our sense of purpose, existence, spiritual self, identity, soul, and energetic connections.

Challenge the default settings, limiting beliefs and/or negative habits.
If any of the above two answers include limiting beliefs or default settings, how can you challenge these beliefs or defaults? What more positive habits can be substituted?

Identify the root need(s) and/or desire(s).

How can you remove, redirect, heal or shift this energy to fit with your desired experience? Write out new ways of being, thinking, feeling and doing that better serves you.

Use this space to free write. Let your thoughts flow freely until you feel you have nothing else to say or write.

Identify the negative habit or cycle you wish to break.

How does this cycle or habit make you feel?
List all the emotions, positive and negative.

What thoughts do you notice that pertain to this cycle or habit?

What actions and/or ways of being are part of this cycle or habit?

Identify any emotional attachments present.
This is any emotional gratification the habit or cycle gives you.

Identify any physical attachments present.
This is any material gain or bodily sensation the habit or cycle gives you.

Identify any mental attachments present.
This is any reinforcement of beliefs or thoughts pertaining to the habit or cycle.

Identify any spiritual attachments present.
This is any emotional, physical or mental gratification or/or reinforcement pertaining to spiritual, energetic or religious experiences or practices. It extends to our sense of purpose, existence, spiritual self, identity, soul, and energetic connections.

Challenge the default settings, limiting beliefs and/or negative habits.
If any of the above two answers include limiting beliefs or default settings, how can you challenge these beliefs or defaults? What more positive habits can be substituted?

Identify the root need(s) and/or desire(s).

How can you remove, redirect, heal or shift this energy to fit with your desired experience? Write out new ways of being, thinking, feeling and doing that better serves you.

Use this space to free write. Let your thoughts flow freely until you feel you have nothing else to say or write.

Identify the negative habit or cycle you wish to break.

How does this cycle or habit make you feel?
List all the emotions, positive and negative.

What thoughts do you notice that pertain to this cycle or habit?

What actions and/or ways of being are part of this cycle or habit?

Identify any emotional attachments present.
This is any emotional gratification the habit or cycle gives you.

Identify any physical attachments present.
This is any material gain or bodily sensation the habit or cycle gives you.

Identify any mental attachments present.
This is any reinforcement of beliefs or thoughts pertaining to the habit or cycle.

Identify any spiritual attachments present.
This is any emotional, physical or mental gratification or/or reinforcement pertaining to spiritual, energetic or religious experiences or practices. It extends to our sense of purpose, existence, spiritual self, identity, soul, and energetic connections.

Challenge the default settings, limiting beliefs and/or negative habits.
If any of the above two answers include limiting beliefs or default settings, how can you challenge these beliefs or defaults? What more positive habits can be substituted?

Identify the root need(s) and/or desire(s).

How can you remove, redirect, heal or shift this energy to fit with your desired experience? Write out new ways of being, thinking, feeling and doing that better serves you.

Use this space to free write. Let your thoughts flow freely until you feel you have nothing else to say or write.

List any unhealthy attachments you had to your ex.

This can be any attachments at all. This question is to give you another perspective in case you missed something. If nothing in addition to what you wrote above comes to mind, skip this question.

How can you remove, redirect or correct these unhealthy attachments in future relationships?

List any unhealthy attachments your ex had with you that you are now aware of.

How did you handle these unhealthy attachments you may have had or that your ex had?

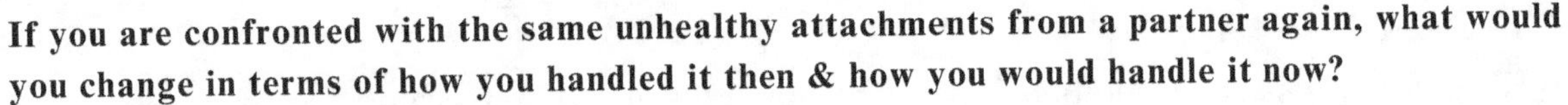

If you are confronted with the same unhealthy attachments from a partner again, what would you change in terms of how you handled it then & how you would handle it now?

Are there any patterns or red flags you now recognize that were indications of these unhealthy attachments whether from you or your ex?

Extra Space or Come Back Later

Use these next few pages as additional space or if you feel you need to repeat this section.

Identify the negative habit or cycle you wish to break.

How does this cycle or habit make you feel?
List all the emotions, positive and negative.

What thoughts do you notice that pertain to this cycle or habit?

What actions and/or ways of being are part of this cycle or habit?

Identify any emotional attachments present.
This is any emotional gratification the habit or cycle gives you.

Identify any physical attachments present.
This is any material gain or bodily sensation the habit or cycle gives you.

Identify any mental attachments present.
This is any reinforcement of beliefs or thoughts pertaining to the habit or cycle.

Identify any spiritual attachments present.
This is any emotional, physical or mental gratification or/or reinforcement pertaining to spiritual, energetic or religious experiences or practices. It extends to our sense of purpose, existence, spiritual self, identity, soul, and energetic connections.

Challenge the default settings, limiting beliefs and/or negative habits.
If any of the above two answers include limiting beliefs or default settings, how can you challenge these beliefs or defaults? What more positive habits can be substituted?

Identify the root need(s) and/or desire(s).

How can you remove, redirect, heal or shift this energy to fit with your desired experience? Write out new ways of being, thinking, feeling and doing that better serves you.

Use this space to free write. Let your thoughts flow freely until you feel you have nothing else to say or write.

Identify the negative habit or cycle you wish to break.

How does this cycle or habit make you feel?
List all the emotions, positive and negative.

What thoughts do you notice that pertain to this cycle or habit?

What actions and/or ways of being are part of this cycle or habit?

Identify any emotional attachments present.
This is any emotional gratification the habit or cycle gives you.

Identify any physical attachments present.
This is any material gain or bodily sensation the habit or cycle gives you.

Identify any mental attachments present.
This is any reinforcement of beliefs or thoughts pertaining to the habit or cycle.

Identify any spiritual attachments present.
This is any emotional, physical or mental gratification or/or reinforcement pertaining to spiritual, energetic or religious experiences or practices. It extends to our sense of purpose, existence, spiritual self, identity, soul, and energetic connections.

Challenge the default settings, limiting beliefs and/or negative habits.
If any of the above two answers include limiting beliefs or default settings, how can you challenge these beliefs or defaults? What more positive habits can be substituted?

Identify the root need(s) and/or desire(s).

How can you remove, redirect, heal or shift this energy to fit with your desired experience? Write out new ways of being, thinking, feeling and doing that better serves you.

Use this space to free write. Let your thoughts flow freely until you feel you have nothing else to say or write.

Identify the negative habit or cycle you wish to break.

How does this cycle or habit make you feel?
List all the emotions, positive and negative.

What thoughts do you notice that pertain to this cycle or habit?

What actions and/or ways of being are part of this cycle or habit?

Identify any emotional attachments present.
This is any emotional gratification the habit or cycle gives you.

Identify any physical attachments present.
This is any material gain or bodily sensation the habit or cycle gives you.

Identify any mental attachments present.
This is any reinforcement of beliefs or thoughts pertaining to the habit or cycle.

Identify any spiritual attachments present.
This is any emotional, physical or mental gratification or/or reinforcement pertaining to spiritual, energetic or religious experiences or practices. It extends to our sense of purpose, existence, spiritual self, identity, soul, and energetic connections.

Challenge the default settings, limiting beliefs and/or negative habits.
If any of the above two answers include limiting beliefs or default settings, how can you challenge these beliefs or defaults? What more positive habits can be substituted?

Identify the root need(s) and/or desire(s).

How can you remove, redirect, heal or shift this energy to fit with your desired experience? Write out new ways of being, thinking, feeling and doing that better serves you.

Use this space to free write. Let your thoughts flow freely until you feel you have nothing else to say or write.

The negative karmic cycles, influences, unhealed wounds, lack of healthy boundaries and attachments others have are not our responsibility to resolve for them. We also cannot force someone to deal with them, heal them or do things differently before they are ready or want to. That being said, we may not be able to entirely avoid these things either. Especially when we are choosing to be in a relationship with someone. Everyone is human and has their own way of confronting challenges. Inevitably, you may come into contact with or be impacted by your partner's negative baggage or their approach to problem solving.

So how do you reclaim your power when a situation like the above mentioned rears its ugly head? You take accountability. Not for the responsibilities of the other person, but for how you react. You can create an open line of healthy communication, provide healthy support and create healthy boundaries. Go back to chapter six if you need a recap on healthy support.

Before we go any further though, let's define what healthy boundaries are and what they are not.

What are healthy boundaries?

Healthy boundaries are the intentional limits you set to safeguard your wants, needs, limits, priorities, trust, wellbeing, peace and values. They can be used in all kinds of relationships. Consider them like protective guardrails guiding you along the road of emotional, physical, spiritual and mental well-being. These boundaries enable you to establish clear parameters regarding what holds significance in your life and what aligns with your best interests. They define what is acceptable and unacceptable for your personal growth and overall health.

What are not healthy boundaries?

When discussing healthy boundaries, it's essential to dive into the nuances of what constitutes "healthy" and what it means to prioritize "yourself."

Firstly, the term "healthy" in the context of boundaries suggests that these limits should be established with a holistic consideration for your well-being. This entails setting boundaries that align with your physical, emotional, spiritual and mental health needs, as well as your values, goals, priorities and personal growth. Healthy boundaries are not meant to be punitive or restrictive but rather serve as safeguards to promote self-respect, overall self esteem, accountability, trust and positive relationships. Boundaries that disregard your needs or perpetuate harmful dynamics are not healthy boundaries. Whether too rigid or too lenient, boundaries that fail to strike a balance can impede personal growth and hinder healthy interactions with others.

The emphasis on "yourself" underscores the agency and responsibility you hold in establishing and maintaining boundaries. Healthy boundaries are created with the intention to support your wellbeing **not** to deprive, control, punish or harm someone else. Setting boundaries is an act of self-care and self-advocacy, requiring introspection and assertiveness. Although being comfortable saying no is a key part of having and maintaining healthy boundaries, healthy boundaries are less about telling other people no and more about defining what you are saying no to in order to support yourself. It's about recognizing and honoring your limits, voicing your preferences, and asserting your rights in relationships and interactions as well as honoring the boundaries of others. Regular self-assessment is crucial to ensure that your boundaries remain aligned with your evolving needs and circumstances. By staying attuned to your inner compass and honoring your boundaries, you empower yourself to cultivate healthier connections and experiences.

Healthy boundaries are a cornerstone of self-care and healthy relationships. They reflect a commitment to prioritizing your well-being while fostering mutual respect and understanding in your interactions with others. By embracing the principles of healthy boundaries and nurturing a compassionate relationship with yourself, you lay the foundation for a more fulfilling and balanced life.

Communicating Healthy Boundaries

Whether you are on the receiving end or you are the one enforcing the healthy boundary, a little communication can go a long way.

If you are on the receiving end, it can help to communicate openly and honestly with your partner about the boundary they are enforcing. Try to be open minded and ask questions that will help you understand the intention behind the boundary and the needs of your partner. Remember, healthy boundaries are meant to make the relationship stronger, not punish you or control you. By respecting other people's healthy boundaries you are helping to ensure their wellbeing and self respect is being honored. In turn, you are supporting a healthy relationship and the overall health of your partner. When your partner is working to do and uphold what is best for them, it is also in your best interest as then your partner is free to be the best version of themselves with you. The same goes for anyone else in your life enforcing healthy boundaries.

When communicating boundaries it is essential that you are calm, as kind as possible, firm, direct and clear about your expectations. If you are met with hurt feelings from the other person, be kind but remain firm. It can help to tell them these boundaries are meant to strengthen the relationship. If being firm is something you struggle with, try to keep your sentences direct and simple. You don't need to over explain yourself

Being Assertive Does NOT Make You An Asshole

Being assertive means you are being firm on your stance, but being assertive does not mean you are automatically being an asshole. You are only an asshole if you say things and behave in a way in which an asshole would.

The intention behind being assertive and being an asshole is different. Being assertive has an intention to be clear, firm and direct. Being an asshole has an intention to be arrogant or to hurt the feelings of someone else. Remember, you are not responsible for the reactions of other people. You can be assertive and still remain kind.

Healthy Boundaries Can Sometimes Feel Like Rejection

If healthy boundaries have been lacking in your life, the lives of those in your life or if there is a shift in boundaries due to a change in needs, values or priorities, healthy boundaries can sometimes feel like punishment, rejection, abandonment or being told no.Whether you are on the receiving end or you are the one speaking up, the process of shifting, communicating and maintaining healthy boundaries can sometimes feel uncomfortable and come with a lot of strong emotions. Each individual person is the only one that will know for sure what boundaries are best for them. With that in mind, boundaries should not be defined or dictated by the reactions or opinions of others. In fact, in most cases, if healthy boundaries are met with a strong reaction, it's a good indication that boundary was necessary.

Keep in mind too, that healthy boundaries are intended to protect your wellbeing, your peace and self respect. This means that you may need to be more assertive with some people over others and there may be some people in your life who you do not need to set the boundary with.

Consequences For Breaking Boundaries.

Part of maintaining healthy boundaries means that there should be consequences for those who do not respect your boundaries. These consequences should not be intended to punish the other person, but to keep you on track, honor your self support and hold the other person accountable for their actions. Continued disrespect for boundaries is a violation of trust, privacy, respect and can be an indication that there is a major misalignment in values and priorities. When establishing your boundaries, get clear with yourself on your course of action should those boundaries go disrespected.

You Teach People How To Treat You Through How You Treat You

The relationship you cultivate with yourself stands as the most profound and influential connection you will ever experience. This dynamic shapes every facet of your life—your thoughts, perceptions, emotions, and decisions. Nurturing a positive relationship with your inner self through the establishment of healthy boundaries is crucial. Allowing disrespect or devaluation is a disservice to your well-being and your immense potential. Your healthy boundaries not only serve

as a guidebook for others on how to treat you but also reflect the support you extend to your self-esteem and overall wellbeing. Consistently upholding these boundaries is paramount; allowing them to be overlooked or disrespected conveys a message of undervaluing your own worth and self-respect. This unintentionally teaches others that negative treatment is acceptable, perpetuating a cycle of disrespect both from others and from yourself. Honoring your boundaries is essential to fortify your self-worth and overall self esteem. It also helps establish clear expectations for the treatment you deserve.

Healthy Boundaries, Your Peace, Your Self Respect & Worth Should NOT Be Negotiable.

It is for the reasons above that your boundaries should NOT BE NEGOTIABLE and you should not allow them to be used as bargaining chips. If you clearly communicate your boundaries and are met with constant justifications, negotiations, rationalizations and apologies, this person is attempting to manipulate you and/or break your boundaries down. This is not love. This is not respect. Compromise and sacrifice are not the same thing. Real love will not ask you to sacrifice yourself in these ways. There are also more ways to give and receive love than through the act of sacrifice. Sacrifice is not a measuring stick for love.

When you do not maintain your healthy boundaries, the foundations of your boundaries begin to fade until you can no longer delineate where the boundary was in the first place. You slowly begin to accept more and more mistreatment until you begin to believe that is what you deserve. You have to be your own advocate. Nobody will do it for you. It is your responsibility to be there for yourself. To love and respect yourself. You cannot make someone determined to misunderstand you understand. You cannot make someone determined to devalue you value you. You cannot make someone determined to disrespect you respect you. You cannot love someone into loving you. You cannot expect honesty from someone who cannot be honest with themselves. You cannot expect a level of awareness from someone who has yet to understand it. You cannot force someone to value something by giving them more of the things they already do not value. You can, however, remove or limit the access and influence these people have in your life through healthy boundaries.

If you find yourself consistently arguing over boundaries, you have allowed your boundaries to be negotiated. No means no. And that is a complete sentence. No ifs, ands or buts about it.

Providing Your Perfect Candidate Package Will Not Help You Find The Perfect Candidate

Many of us have dedicated considerable thought to what we desire and require in a relationship and a partner, often resulting in what I refer to as the "Ideal Candidate Package." This package represents either a mental or tangible checklist that guides our dating preferences.

When initially establishing healthy boundaries, it's common to fall into the trap of laying out all your expectations in one conversation early on in a relationship, essentially handing over the Ideal Candidate Package to the person you are dating. This might seem like a proactive way to uphold boundaries, but it can backfire if it overshadows the process of genuinely getting to know your partner and their authentic values and priorities. It can also come across as transactional and off putting to someone who could be a real ideal candidate for you.

The key is to communicate your overall intentions clearly from the start about whether you're seeking something casual or serious. This clarity sets a clear expectation without getting into all the specifics. Once this intention has been made clear, it's important to allow space for your partner to reveal their true selves through meaningful conversation and observation. This means you don't hand over all your desires and expectations in one conversation at the beginning of seeing someone. By being present and actively engaging with your partner, you create an environment where they feel comfortable being authentic. This approach minimizes the risk of them pretending to fit your expectations and encourages genuine connection.

Rather than bombarding them with a laundry list of requirements or expectations, focus on listening and asking insightful questions. This enables you to assess compatibility without overwhelming the other person, prematurely boxing them into an idealized image or handing over your ideal candidate package to someone who may not have good intentions. This approach will allow you to quickly assess if this person truly aligns with your desires, values and priorities without the games or pressures that can come with handing over your ideal guidelines.

What happens when the boundaries in a relationship are not the same?

Sometimes healthy compromises or open communication can resolve this issue, but when it doesn't, this is when you have to ask a very important question. Do the values and priorities you have align with your partner, if not completely, in a way in which enough respect exists between the two of you for the difference in values and priorities to be sustainable? Respect is the key word here. You can have a difference in boundaries, opinions, priorities and even certain values so long as you both can respect those differences and the boudaries that go along with them. But if there is no respect and no trust, there is no foundation. Cut your losses. You deserve someone who can meet you with mutual respect

Use Your Emotions As A Guide

When something is out of alignment, your intuition will send you gut feelings and physical feelings of discomfort to let you know. Although getting input from trusted members of your inner circle can prove to be a valuable form of support, only you will truly know what boundaries are best and most healthy for you. Use your emotions as a guide. If you feel unhappy, constantly tired, unfulilled or another negative emotion, take some time to reflect on these feelings. Your feelings are an important guide as to what is and what is not working in your life. Make adjustments as needed and use healthy boundaries to give yourself a stable foundation.

It's Okay To Ask For Help

If you find determining, establishing, maintaining and communicating healthy boundaries especially challenging, you may want to seek help from a licensed professional such as a therapist to help you. Asking for help from the right people and doing all you can to support yourself is a form of self care and self love. Some wounds run deep and it can sometimes be very helpful to gain an unbiased, outside perspective to provide new tools or ways of looking at things.

Outline Your Healthy Boundaries

Now that we grasp the concept of healthy boundaries more clearly, let's examine their effectiveness or lack thereof in your recent relationship. We'll assess which boundaries were upheld and which ones were neglected, and identify the boundaries that should be prioritized going forward.

What are the values, priorities, or needs you feel are important to you in general mentally, physically, spiritually and emotionally?

List any hard outs or limitations in terms of what is and is not acceptable to you in general, in romantic relationships, in non-romantic relationships. Use answers from previous sections to help you.

Make a list of your new healthy boundaries and consequences for breaking these boundaries.

Were any of these values, priorities, limitations, needs and boundaries the same in your previous relationship?

◯ Yes ◯ No

If so, what are some ways you honored them or ways they were effective?

If not, what changes do you now recognize you need or want?

Did you communicate these values, priorities, limitations, needs and boundaries in your last relationship? If not, why? What prevented you from doing so or doing so effectively?

Are any of your reasons for not communicating or not communicating effectively due to limiting beliefs, default settings or low self esteem? If so, what can you do to challenge this and/or better support yourself moving forward?

In what ways did your partner honor and respect these boundaries if applicable?

List any unhealthy boundaries in your last relationship and the reasons they are unhealthy if applicable.

Can any of these unhealthy boundaries be turned into a healthy boundary? If so, list how. If not, what root need or desire did they stem from?

If your healthy boundaries were not respected in the last relationship, why did you allow the boundaries to be disrespected? What attachments might you have had to this decision and how can you remove, heal or realign?

List any areas you need to work on in term of creating and maintaining healthy boundaries.

How can you better support your healthy boundaries moving forward?

Were any of your boundaries ineffective in your last relationship? If so, how and what can you do to make them more effective?

Write any final thoughts you have on healthy boundaries in the space provided below.

MISALIGNMENT

We've explored the concept that alignment involves becoming the version of yourself that not only possesses but also attracts what you truly desire. What we haven't talked about yet is how alignment is most potent when it originates authentically, resonating with the truth of your soul rather than merely reflecting what you think you want. Misalignment, therefore, can manifest in any form that disrupts the harmony between you, your experiences, emotions, or thoughts, and your ultimate truth or desires.

The complexity of misalignment lies in its diverse manifestations – it's not confined to a singular thing, person, or situation. It encompasses everything incongruent with your genuine heart's desires and soul truth. Recognizing misalignment requires skill, awareness, and honesty.

While we've discussed various elements contributing to misalignment, such as perceptions, external validations, fear, coping mechanisms, internal self, limiting beliefs, default settings, attachments, and healthy boundaries, there are additional ways it can manifest in our lives.

Misalignment might occur when the pieces don't coalesce to form a cohesive whole, when inappropriate tools are employed to achieve desired outcomes, when goals are pursued with misguided intentions or methodologies, when you live for others rather than yourself, when you conform to someone else's rules instead of your own, when what you think you want diverges from what you truly need, when you react instead of act with intention, or when you engage in self-sabotage. Essentially, misalignment arises when pursuits are inauthentic on any level. It transpires when something fails to align with the genuine fulfillment of your soul or your highest, most gratifying reality. Energetic transactions contribute to misalignment when invested in the wrong places, people, or things.

For a deeper comprehension of misalignment, let's explore its connection to the dynamics of attraction.

Emotional Attraction

Emotional attraction encompasses the deep satisfaction, fulfillment, trust, support, vulnerability, and sense of connection we find enticing in someone or something. It encompasses the ways in which emotions are shared, expressed, or evoked, as well as the cognitive processes related to emotion and establishing emotional bonds.

Physical Attraction

Physical attraction pertains to the allure we feel towards physical appearance, material possessions, and their associations. It encompasses perceptions of success, wealth, attractiveness, sex appeal, style, and more. Additionally, it involves the stimulation of the five senses—taste, touch, sight, hearing, and smell.

Mental Attraction

Mental attraction refers to the attraction we feel towards a particular mode of thinking, understanding, intelligence, or problem-solving. It encompasses the appeal of feeling mentally stimulated and resonating with a specific style of communication.

Spiritual Attraction

Spiritual attraction entails being drawn to values and priorities. This encompasses alignment with spiritual or religious beliefs, morals, life purpose, and energetic resonance with people and things.

The Right Attraction

Our emotional, physical, mental, and spiritual attractions to people, situations, and things significantly shape our desires and preferences. While each form of attraction offers its own advantages, studies indicate that connections rooted in shared values, priorities, and moral compasses tend to foster deeper, more fulfilling relationships.

When our attractions lack spiritual alignment, they can inadvertently lead us into situations or relationships that are misaligned. This underscores the importance of spiritual resonance in our attractions, which brings me to my next point:

Everything You Do Is A Spiritual Practice

As your awareness deepens, so does your alignment. You come to understand that your ability to manifest is constantly active, making every action a spiritual endeavor. Therefore, the more purposeful you are, the more focused your manifestation energies become. Alignment emerges from conscious living, while misalignment often stems from inadvertence or misplaced focus. To live a more purposeful life, we must learn how to slow down and act with intention.

Now that you have a deeper understanding of attractions and misalignment, let's see how they may have effected your last relationship and perpetuated negative karmic cycles.

Decribe your ideal romantic relationship. How would you think, feel, act and be?

___

___

___

___

What values would your ideal relationship be built on?

List your needs and your wants in the relationship.

In what ways, if any, did your last relationship align to and differ from your ideal relationship?

What attractions were present in your last relationship and how did they manifest?

I asked you about attraction in your relationship evaluation. Now that you have come all this way, what are any new revelations you have regarding attraction and what is fulfilling/authentic for you?

List any areas your wants did not align with your needs in your last relationship if applicable. Example: you want someone ambitious but were upset that person was not more present.

List any areas your wants have not aligned with your needs in your life in general if applicable.

How do these realizations change the way you will move forward?

How can you create better alignment between your wants and needs inside and outside of relationships?

Is there anything else you notice that is misaligned in your relationships or in your life?

How can you align more authentically? What do you still need to release, heal or change?

Are there any ways in which you can make more intentional, purposeful or conscious decision in your life and in your relationships?

If you knew without a doubt that your life was fully aligned in all ways to your truest desires and your most authentic truth, what would your life be like? What would it look like? Feel like? What thoughts would you have? What would you be doing? How would you be open and remain open to receiving your desires?

FINAL LESSONS

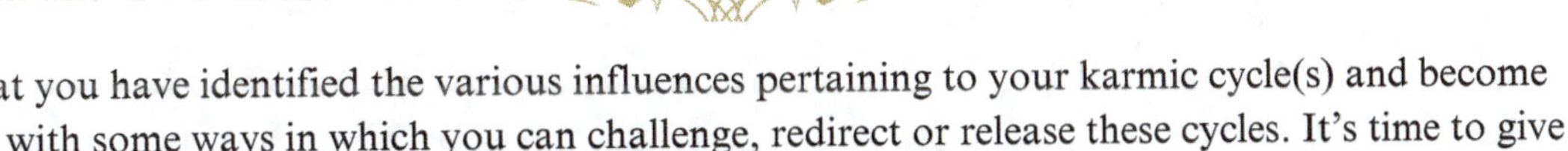

Now that you have identified the various influences pertaining to your karmic cycle(s) and become familiar with some ways in which you can challenge, redirect or release these cycles. It's time to give yourself a pat on the back and recognize how far you have come.

What lesson(s) did you learn in general from this latest relationship? What did your ex teach you about yourself, your needs and your desires?

How can you apply these lessons to your life, your next relationship and to your relationships as a whole?

What have you learn about yourself through this whole process? How can you apply this knowledge to your life?

Are there any other areas that need some realignment? This can be in general, in your relationships, in your perceptions of love, your relationship to self or anything else that comes to mind.

Is there anything left that you still need to release? If so, what and how can you release it?

Is there anything left that you still need to heal? If so, what and how can you heal it?

Is there anything left that you still need to forgive? If so, what and how can you forgive?

Is there anything left that you still need to change? If so, what and how can you change it?

Are there any accomplishments you achieved in general or through this journal process you need to acknowledge?

If there were things that worked, how can you repeat, build upon or level them up moving forward?

Do you have any new perspectives or definitions on love and self love? If so, expand on this.

CREATE YOUR OWN AFFIRMATIONS

CREATE A LIST OF AFFIRMATIONS BASED ON THE ANSWERS YOU GAVE IN THIS CHAPTER THAT TACKLE ANY PROCESSES THAT NEED ADJUSTMENTS & SUPPORT THE LATEST VERSION OF YOU.

FREE WRITE:

Congratulations! You just completed the hardest section of this journal. Acknowledge your accomplishment and take a moment to reflect on how far you have come.

Use this section to free write about the last chapter or anything else that comes to mind. Keep writing until you feel you have nothing else to say.

A LETTER FOR CLOSURE

Compose a letter addressed to your ex-partner. Rest assured, this letter is meant exclusively for your eyes and serves as a vital part of your healing journey. Within this letter, pour out all the thoughts and feelings you've been wanting to express, without holding back. Write until you've exhausted everything you wish to share.

A LETTER FOR YOU FROM YOU

Compose a letter addressed to yourself, imagining that you are your future self who has fully healed and is living the life you've always envisioned. Write without judgment and without overthinking – simply let the guidance from your higher self flow onto the page. What does this version of you have to say to you right now? What guidance can you impart?

CHAPTER *Twelve*

FALLING IN LOVE WITH YOU

BUILDING A STRONG FOUNDATION FOR SELF

Your relationship with yourself is the foundation for all the other interactions and relationships in your life which is why it is crucial to make your relationship to self a priority.

In this section, we will concentrate on developing that foundation, enhancing overall self-esteem, exploring methods to balance energies, nurturing trust both internally and externally, and empowering yourself to prioritize your happiness. Overall, this section is designed to help you fall in love with yourself or reignite that love within you.

BUILDING SELF ESTEEM

As we discussed in the last chapter, self esteem is the culmination of your self confidence, self acceptance, self worth and self love. You know you have a strong self esteem if you hold more positive thoughts and feelings towards yourself than negative. The more you can cultivate a strong self esteem from within, the less influenced you will be by negativity or perceived negativity. The stronger foundation you create for yourself, the deeper understanding, acceptance, respect, awareness and love you hold for yourself.

Let's take a look at each piece of self esteem in more detail. The answers you provided in the last chapter will give you some insight as to specific pain points you may be experiencing with your relationship to self in each of these areas.

SELF CONFIDENCE

To give a quick recap on self confidence, self confidence is trusting in your abilities and decision making. Although self confidence extends to confidence we have in a set of skills, for the context of this introspective journey, when I mention self-confidence, I am specifically addressing your confidence in your relationship with yourself.

The central theme when it comes to confidence is trust. But how can you determine if you truly trust yourself, and what does trust really entail?

Trust involves believing in the reliability, truthfulness, competence, character, safety, and strength of a person or circumstance. Just as with support and attachments, trust can be broken down into four primary pillars: emotional, mental, physical, and spiritual. Let's take a look at each of these pillars of trust in greater detail.

4 PILLARS OF TRUST

Emotional	Mental
Emotional trust is feeling safe to express emotions and be emotionally vulnerable. It extends to the ability to support a positive and healthy emotional wellbeing	Mental trust encompasses feeling secure in expressing ideas and having confidence in decision-making abilities. It extends to the ability to support a positive and healthy mental wellbeing
Physical	**Spiritual**
Overall, physical trust is about feeling secure and confident in the physical world. Physical trust involves feeling safe in physical surroundings and safe from bodily harm. It also includes trust in the reliability and safety of the materials in your physical world and the ability to care for physical wants and needs.	Spiritual trust involves placing confidence in the strength and reliability of values, priorities and character. It extends to trusting in energies, intuition, and faith. While faith can encompass literal spirituality or religion, it also entails having trust in positive outcomes even when it seems unlikely.

These four pillars of trust play a vital role not only in your own self-confidence but also in shaping the quality of your relationships. When trust is firmly established in these areas, it lays the foundation for stronger and more enriching connections.

Trust in oneself—physically, mentally, emotionally, and spiritually—lays the groundwork for trusting others and being trusted in return. This mutual trust fosters deeper bonds, facilitates open communication, and cultivates a sense of security within relationships. When individuals feel confident and secure in themselves and their connections, it paves the way for greater intimacy, understanding and fulfillment in their interactions with others.

ESTABLISHING VALUES AND PRIORITIES

Before we dive into how to establish trust in each of the four pillars, you must first define and understand what you value and prioritize in these four areas of your life.

What do you value and prioritize when it comes to emotional trust in yourself and with others?

What do you value and prioritize when it comes to mental trust in yourself and with others?

What do you value and prioritize when it comes to physical trust in yourself and with others?

What do you value and prioritize when it comes to spiritual trust in yourself and with others?

What values and priorities do you look for in your ideal partner?

What value and priorities do you look for in the character of your ideal partner?

What do you value and prioritize in your own character?

What do you value and prioritize when it comes to yourself in general?

What do you value and prioritize in your life in general?

BUILDING TRUST

Trust is the ultimate groundwork for the foundation in all relationships. Trust is earned and built over time with consistency. The same is true when it comes to the trust you hold for yourself and the confidence you have in that trust. In order to build a strong self confidence, you must work to prove to yourself that you are a safe space for yourself, that you are reliable, consistent, true to yourself and competent in your dealings with yourself. As you create a strong consistency in trust for yourself, you create a resilience that allows you to tackle more complex challenges with more confidence and less stress.

Using the values you listed, answer the following questions to help improve your self confidence in yourself.

Evaluate where your level of trust stands in each pillar of trust with yourself. Are there areas you feel confident? Areas that could improve?

How can you honor the emotional values and priorities you listed in the last group of questions?

What actions and healthy boundaries can you put in place to support your emotional trust for yourself?

What would it take for you to feel like you are an emotionally safe place for yourself?

What actions can you take to develop a sense of self-reliance in meeting your emotional needs and desires? How can you care for yourself emotionally?

How can you improve your understanding, become more aware, create space for, cultivate a deeper connection with, demonstrate greater compassion towards, and respect your emotions?

How can you honor the mental values and priorities you listed in the last group of questions?

What actions and healthy boundaries can you put in place to support your mental trust for yourself?

What steps can you take to build trust in your decision-making abilities, feel confident and secure in your choices, and remain open to new ideas? How can you prioritize your mental well-being?

What actions can you take to develop a sense of self-reliance in meeting your mental health and well being needs and desires? How can you care for yourself mentally?

How can you create an environment for yourself that encourages an open and free flow of ideas?

How can you refine your thinking to improve understanding, increase awareness, and cultivate self-compassionate thought patterns? How can you actively engage in reflective thinking?

List any negative thought patterns you are aware of and then challenge each one below.

How can you honor the physical values and priorities you listed in the last group of questions?

What actions and healthy boundaries can you put in place to support your physical trust for yourself?

What actions can you take to create a sense of physical safety within yourself? How can you prioritize physical self-care?

What steps can you take to develop a sense of self-reliance in meeting all your physical needs and desires?

How can you enhance your comprehension of and raise awareness for your physical needs and desires?

What can you do to support your physical health?

SOME KEY ASPECTS OF THE SPIRITUAL TRUST PILLAR

Before we dive into the spiritual pillar questions, let's explore some fundamental aspects of the spiritual trust pillar and their impact on your self-confidence.

Higher Self:

Your higher self is your soul and/or divine spirit.

Spirit Team:

Your spirit team consists of your spirit guides, angels, ancestors, friend or family who have passed on, the universal energies, your higher self, intuition and the ascended masters.

Intuition:

What exactly is intuition? It's the serene and loving inner voice and knowing that guides you toward alignment with your higher self. Intuition helps you interpret the guidance received from the spiritual realm and your spirit team. It also helps you tune in to the energies that are surrounding you.

Developing a connection with your higher self and spirit team involves nurturing your intuition. It's a crucial step in fostering spiritual trust and improving overall well-being. This process not only helps in building trust and faith but also in cultivating an abundant mindset.

Everyone possesses the capacity to access divine guidance at any given time. Your higher self and spirit team are continuously available, tirelessly advocating for your highest good. Yet, refining and deepening this connection might necessitate practice. Intuition is a skill, not a magical trait reserved for a select few. Those with a heightened intuition aren't inherently more mystical. They have simply honed their ability through practice in recognizing and heeding its whispers.

The more you listen to and trust your intuition, the more potent that inner voice and sense of knowing becomes. Yet, when self-confidence is lacking, this voice often goes unheard and doubts may hinder you from following its guidance.

YOUR INTUITION NEVER LIES & IS SAFE GUIDANCE

It will always be in your best interest to heed your intuition. Your higher self embodies your most divine essence. It offers unconditional love and unwavering support. For this reason, the communication your receive from your intuition will never lie or lead you astray. It is communication and guidance coming directly from your highest of high. Your intuition provides safe guidance, but it's essential to learn to recognize, differentiate and follow it in order to fully benefit from its wisdom.

COMMUNICATION & INTUITION

Just as every person communicates uniquely, so does their intuition. It's important to learn to recognize when your intuition is speaking and interpret its messages.

The Voice of Your Intuition:

Your intuition will communicate its messages consistently and with love. Your intuition will never talk down to you or make you feel inferior. This stark contrast distinguishes the voice of intuition from that of your inner critic.

Other Ways Your Intuition or Spirit Team May Communicate:

Apart from the serene and affectionate voice I mentioned earlier, your intuition or spirit team may communicate with you in various other ways. You may not be aware of it, but your intuition and your spirit team are constantly communicating with you all the time. Messages and communication will always show up in ways that resonate with you and your lifestyle. Here are some examples:

- Reoccurring signs, patterns and synchronicities such as angel numbers, spirit animals, feathers, colors, synchronistic conversations, reoccurring thought or idea patterns, repeating themes, words or symbols, unexpected conversations with strangers that feel like spiritual experiences etc.
- Visions and dreams through mediation, sleep or prayer.
- Some people believe that experiencing déjà vu confirms that they are on the right path. It's thought that the events triggering déjà vu serve as signpost reminders set up by one's spiritual self before being born on Earth.
- Spiritual downloads which are transmissions of spiritual information, messages, wisdom, or knowledge that occur beyond the realm of logical comprehension.
- Energy, auras or light.
- Technology interruptions or glitches.
- Blessings in disguise.
- Unexplainable feeling of knowing something you couldn’t possibly know.
- Sudden breakthroughs or an influx of inspiration.
- Physical sensations such as feelings of peace, nostalgia, itchiness or discomfort.
- Overwhelming doubt or bad gut feeling.
- By recognizing these significant patterns and contemplating your thoughts and emotions about them, both at the moment of occurrence and immediately afterwards, you can decode the messages they carry. Take a moment to pause and reflect. Sometimes, a quick internet search can offer common interpretations that provide additional information. Remember to always take what resonates and leave what doesn’t. Not every single interpretation of every message is for you. Remember, if it feels wrong or off it likely is.

REPEAT MESSAGES

The messages you receive manifest in various forms not only because synchronicities occur uniquely to you, but also because they originate from different members of your spirit team, each with its distinct communication style. The repetition of a specific message often indicates the heightened attention your spirit team wants to bring to it and/or the urgency pertaining to time-sensitive matters. Repeat synchronicities are also the universe's way of indicating to you what energies you are attracting. These energies create patterns that serve as a mirror that reflects back to you what you are communicating to the universe. When a message is conveyed through diverse forms, it increases the likelihood you will comprehend and recognize it as synchronicity rather than mere coincidence.

RECOGNIZING PATTERNS

The Rule of 3: When you're initially navigating the process of communicating with and trusting your spirit team, discerning between signs and coincidences can pose a challenge. Personally, I no longer believe in coincidences. Through my journey, I've realized that although occurrences may appear random, nothing truly happens by accident. However, attaining this level of spiritual trust didn't happen overnight. This is where the Rule of 3 proves invaluable in identifying synchronistic patterns in your life, serving as a valuable spiritual tool you can revisit whenever needed. The Rule of 3 is straightforward: when you encounter something that seems like a potential message, ask your spirit team to present it two more times if it's something worth your attention. Why three? Once might be chance, twice coincidence, but three times? That's a pattern.

Track Your Synchronicities: I'll be honest. This is such a simple yet profound spiritual tip, one that I overlooked for years due to its simplicity. I never imagined that such a straightforward practice could have such a profound impact on my life. Here's the thing: when you track your synchronicities, the patterns become glaringly obvious, making you wonder why you ever doubted them in the first place. Then, upon reviewing the list you've compiled each day, even more obvious patterns emerge. This has led to significant breakthroughs in my life and has facilitated a direct line of communication with the universe, my intuition, and other members of my spirit team.

TUNING IN AND OUT TO ADJUST SPIRITUAL SENSITIVITY

Whether you are a beginner or seasoned in your spiritual journey, it's beneficial to understand how to regulate your sensitivity to the energies and spiritual communication surrounding you. This regulation of spiritual sensitivity is commonly known as "tuning in and out." Tuning in and out serves as a valuable tool for maintaining healthy spiritual boundaries, particularly for those with strong intuition or empathic abilities. Establishing these boundaries is crucial for spiritual self-care. Excessive spiritual energy or information can lead to feelings of exhaustion, fatigue, or overwhelm.

There are various methods for tuning in and out, but I'll share the approach that has been most effective for me. While I can't guarantee it works the same for everyone, I find myself constantly engaged in spiritual communication and deeply attuned to the energies surrounding me. To tune in and out, I envision myself enveloped in an invisible, perpetual energetic shield. This shield's energy derives from divine creative energy rather than my personal energy, ensuring it never requires recharging and doesn't wane with my personal energy levels. When I desire to decrease the intensity of this energetic field to welcome more information, I visualize a dial in my mind ranging from zero to one hundred. Zero indicates no energetic field at all, while one hundred signifies shields are fully activated, rendering them impenetrable. I adjust the shield's strength to accommodate varying levels of incoming information. On a daily basis, I set the dial to my personal "normal" sensitivity level.

ASKING FOR CLARITY AND ASKING FOR HELP

Your intuition, your higher self and spirit team is there for you whenever you need. If you feel confused or need assistance all you need to do is ask for help or clarity. One way I have found helpful to ask for this is by simply saying, "Spirit team and higher self, please send me clear and gentle signs as to where I should go from here and what I should be doing."

Yes, No & Neutral:

You can enhance your communication and understanding with your higher self
and intuition by requesting clear and consistent signs for yes, no, and neutral answers to your questions. This can be achieved through practices like stillness, meditation or prayer. Once you reach a state of tranquility during these practices, request each sign from your intuition and higher self individually. You'll recognize this state of calm when you are aware you can adjust your body or seek a more comfortable position, yet you remain content and have no desire to move. Pay attention to any physical sensations in your body. For instance, does your right arm tingle for yes, do you feel a sense of dread in your gut for no, or do you see a flash of blue in your mind's eye for neutral? Allow the communication to unfold naturally, embracing whatever form it takes. Next, test out this new method of communication in low-pressure situations over the following month. Ask your intuition and higher self to provide yes, no, or neutral answers to various trivial matters in which you have no personal investment. For example, you might inquire about parking in the left or right spot or choosing between two sweaters. It's important to select questions where you don't have a personal stake, as this ensures you'll consistently follow through with the guidance received. Ignoring the communication in situations where you're personally invested won't aid in strengthening your trust in this divine guidance. Throughout this period, pay attention to any emerging patterns, as they may offer valuable insights. You may also come to realize that your higher self provides you with unforeseen benefits or additional abundance when you heed the guidance.

INTUITION WILL NOT ALWAYS FEEL RATIONAL

As we have established, intuition is the communication you receive from your higher self. This means that your intuition will not always feel rational. It often conveys very subtle information from a perspective beyond our current logical understanding. Therefore, following your intuition may sometimes necessitate taking a leap of faith and placing a considerable amount of trust in its guidance.

Try not to overthink when you receive intuitive messages like these. Typically, the first instinct, thought or decision that feels the most natural and right is the correct answers even if the reason is unclear at the time.

INTUITION AND DOUBT

Doubt can play a complex role in intuitive messages; sometimes, it can be a message itself, while at other times, it can hinder intuitive communication. It's normal to experience a sliver of doubt when dealing with intuitive messages that don't seem rational. Your human mind may struggle to fully grasp your spiritual experiences.

However, when doubt becomes overwhelming, it may signal a misalignment or a warning from your intuition. Pay close attention to this sensation, especially if it intensifies and coincides with increased synchronicities. This could indicate the need to pause and reflect before proceeding with intention.

FOMO: FEAR OF MISSING OUT

Doubt, especially when it emerges in situations where we strongly desire a specific outcome, can lead us to disregard crucial intuitive guidance out of fear of making a mistake. Particularly before we've developed a strong sense of trust in our spiritual self and team, it's common to ignore intuitive messages because we fear missing out if our intuition turns out to be incorrect.

However, it's important to recognize that intuition is inherently accurate. If something feels off or wrong, it likely is. There's no need to spend time analyzing or investigating why or how it's off or wrong. By doing so, you set yourself up for getting confirmation, but it also sets you up for any other negative circumstances that come with it. In my experience, you often get confirmation later down the line while still dodging a bullet if you just choose to trust and have faith in the intuitive message right off the bat. As you cultivate trust in your intuition, doubt and fear surrounding following intuitive guidance diminish because you develop confidence.

Remember, you can't miss out on anything meant for you, but you can delay it by staying in circumstances that are not for you. Your intuition wouldn't prompt a negative instinct about a circumstance if there were something to actually miss out on. Avoid making decisions driven by fear, and instead, trust in your intuition to guide you toward what truly serves your highest good.

PARNOIA VS INTUITION

If you're grappling with listening to your intuition, you might be thinking something like, "Well Blake, that's all well and good, but how do I distinguish between my intuition and just being paranoid?"

The key lies in consistency and the nature of doubt. Your intuition will consistently send you thoughts, feelings, and patterns that signal when something isn't quite right. On the other hand, paranoia tends to be inconsistent and stems from fears, worries, anxieties, triggers, and unresolved wounds that don't accurately reflect reality. Paranoia often involves unfounded or unjustified suspicion. With intuition, even if the whole picture isn't clear, there will be more consistent patterns to support it. There will be a sense of knowing for a fact something is off but maybe not being able to put your finger on exactly what.

Earlier, I described intuition as a knowing. Another significant difference between paranoia and intuition is that intuitive doubt will feel right. It will feel like knowing without knowing exactly how you know even if there is a sliver of doubt present. Paranoia will feel more like fear, complete uncertainty, grasping at straws or victimization.

YOU RESIDE IN WHAT YOU DECIDE

You reside in the polarity of energies, whether large or small, positive or negative, that you decide to feed in your life. Whatever you feed and nurture is what will grow. This is true in manifestation and true when it comes to intuition. If you feed doubt when it comes to your intuition, then more doubt will grow and the less you will trust in your intuition. If you feed faith and trust in your intuition, then you will build confidence in your intuition. Part of learning how to have and maintain spiritual trust in yourself is trusting in your ability to reside where you intentionally decide.

How can you honor the spiritual values and priorities you listed in the first group of questions in this chapter?

What actions and healthy boundaries can you put in place to support your spiritual trust for yourself?

Just like you should have healthy boundaries with your friends and family, you should have healthy boundaries with your spirit team. For example, if your Great Aunt Julian has been appearing in your dreams every night for two weeks, urging you to deliver messages to her cat that you took in after her passing, and this has left you exhausted each day due to a lack of proper sleep, it may be time to establish some spiritual boundaries. It's an extreme and amusing example, but spiritual boundaries are often neglected when discussing spiritual wellbeing. Spiritual boundaries can also be simple things, such as telling your partner, "Hey babe, don't interrupt me while I'm meditating." Write out any spiritual boundaries that would help you build and maintain spiritual trust for yourself and with your spirit team.

What would it take for you to feel like you are a spiritually safe place for yourself?

What would it take for you to feel like you can rely on yourself to take care of all your spiritual needs and wants?

How can you enhance your comprehension and raise awareness for your spiritual needs?

What can you do to support your spiritual wellbeing?

How clear are you on your spitiual values and priorities? If this needs work, how can you better define this area to give more clarity?

How can you strengthen your spiritual values and priorities? What spiritual practices can you create for yourself?

How connected do you feel to your higher self, intuition, your spirit guides, and/or the universal energies? What influences are present?

What can you do to strengthen the relationship with the above?

How well do you know your spiritual self and what can you do to build a stronger relationship and trust with this side of you?

What would it take for you to fully trust your intution and know when it is speaking to you?

Do you recognize any specific signs, feelings or sensations when your intuition speaks to you? How can you strengthen this communication?

How confident are you in your belief that the universe, your higher self and your spirit guides, love, support, and will assist you?

How strong is your faith that things will work out for the best no matter what and the universe is always working for you?

How can you increase your trust and faith in the above two questions?

TRACK YOUR SYNCHRONICITIES

Monitor your synchronicities and intuitive messages over the course of a week to deepen your spiritual connection and strengthen your trust. Consider recording these occurrences in your phone while on the move and transferring them here later. Take moments each day to contemplate and jot down any recurring messages you receive from these signs. At the week's end, reflect on all the messages gathered and how this practice has impacted your sense of connection and well-being.

MONDAY	TUESDAY	WEDNESDAY	THURSDAY

FRIDAY	SATURDAY	SUNDAY	NOTES

SELF WORTH

To give a quick recap on self worth, self worth is the valuation you place on yourself, your capabilities and worthiness to receive good. But what determines your value and how is it calculated?

This section will help you understand self worth on a deeper level and how to cultivate it within yourself so that you have a strong sense of self worth.

HOW TO DETERMINE SELF WORTH

In my opinion, self worth is the hardest part of the inner self to comprehend, heal and master. A deficiency in self-worth serves as the primary cause of numerous issues both individually and within relationships, as well as a significant factor in low self-esteem. It has such a substantial influence because self worth determines our deep seated perception of ourselves, who we believe we are and how much happiness we believe we deserve.

The problem many people face when it comes to self worth is they have been conditioned by outside influences to use the wrong measurements to calculate their worthiness. This causes many people to tie their self worth to the outside validations, perceptions and outcomes of these measurements and labels.

LABELING

Let's talk about labeling. Labeling is when we place a value on something based on relative, perceived value. Value, in general, is relative. It is determined by the polarity of positive or negative feelings and thoughts surrounding something. The more positive the feelings and thoughts, the more value it has. The more negative, the less value.

We use labeling to place perceived value on things like society, religion, gender, sexuality, age, occupation, financial standing, relationship status, social status, physical appearance, our past etc. However, much like how a billionaire might view a million dollars as a modest sum while someone struggling financially might see it as life-changing, these labels hold value only because we assign it to them. And this value is relative, varying with each individual's perspective.

Our self worth is the same. We determine it by our perception and we often use the labeling we place on things and people to determine our worth. Things like society, religion, gender, sexuality, age, occupation, financial standing, relationship status, social status, our past, the perceived worth of others, accomplishments, other's opinions of us, how many friends we have, our social media following, our weight etc. can all impact how we perceive our worth.

Guess what though? None of the things I listed above have any bearing once so ever on your value nor should they be used to measure your value. Some of these things can amplify who you already are, but they are not a part of what makes you worthy or not worthy.

THE UNIVERSE DID NOT FUCK UP

The universe did not fuck up when you were created. You were not placed on this earth as a salvation project. The universe didn't attach any conditions when it bestowed upon you its unconditional love, and it granted you free will because it believes in your capacity to achieve greatness. Everything that exists has a purpose, therefore you have value simply by existing.

To give you some food for thought, consider this: I remember having this revelation in high school anatomy class and, honestly, it blew my mind.There are billions of people that populate earth. On average, each woman will have a couple million eggs in their lifetime while each man will produce trillions of sperm in their lifetime. I'm not a math genius, but that means the odds of you being created exactly as you are with all exact specifications are...well, crazy as fuck! This means your existence is no accident and the fact that you exist is a miracle in itself.

Make no mistakes, your creation was not a mistake. Everything about you was created with intention and purpose. And you were given the gift of deciding how to weild that intention and purpose to impact the world.

WHAT DOES ALL THIS TELL US?

You are worthy because you exist. You are inherently worthy. Period. Full stop. No ifs, ands or buts. No conditions. No stipulations.

But this fact does not override the laws of the universe such as the law of attraction and your free will. This means you are also worthy when and because you decide and choose to be worthy. You are worthy because you think, feel and be worthy. You are worthy because you allow yourself to be worthy. You are worthy by choosing what you are and are not willing to put up with. You are worthy by what you decide to value and prioritize. But above all, you are worthy by how much happiness you decide you deserve regardless of your inherent worthiness.

SO HOW DO YOU DECIDE AND CHOOSE TO BE WORTHY?

Well, you learn to get out of your own way mostly. You learn to release that which is not in alignment and authentic to the deepest truths of who you are. You choose to be kind to yourself and treat yourself with compassion. You stop comparing yourself to others. You decide and choose to be worthy by becoming worthy.

This is the part that trips a lot of people up and causes them to pursue worthiness through labeling. You do not manifest what you want. You manifest what you become. That being said, when I say you decide and choose to be worthy by becoming worthy that doesn't mean you are not worthy and must become worthy. As we have established, you are inherently worthy. What I mean is you have to become the version of yourself who not only knows but BELIEVES you are inherently worthy. This means you must learn how to trust in your worthiness.

TRUSTING IN WORTHINESS

Do you recall my earlier remark about the importance of earning and nurturing trust through consistent actions over time? The same principle applies to your sense of worthiness. The more you champion the version of yourself that acknowledges and embraces your inherent worth, the deeper your trust and confidence in your own value will grow. It entails being the support and advocate for yourself that you seek from others. You must become your own best friend, mentor, and ally, fostering a relationship that nurtures your happiness, self-esteem, and overall well-being. This journey requires introspection and tough questions. Are you creating a safe space within yourself? Just as we assign value to the things we cherish, are you prioritizing your own importance? Are you extending to yourself the same level of care and consideration that you offer to others? Are you aligning your actions with the values you admire in others? If the answer to any of these questions is no, then that means we have some work to do.

Whether or not you truly believe it yet, you deserve all the happiness life has to offer. This group of questions is designed to help you achieve this through inner work focused on worthiness, and, more importantly, will help you make worthiness a part of your daily practice.

What would it take for you to give yourself permission to be happy?

What truly brings you joy and fulfillment without external validation? What do you like doing or enjoy simply for the hell of it?

What is the root energy of what you listed above. How can you incorporate more of that energy into your daily life?

Do you engage in any behaviors towards yourself that you would deem unacceptable if directed towards a close friend? If yes, how can you alter these behaviors?

List any ways that you are unkind to yourself or ways you criticize yourself.

How can you do things differently and be more compassionate with yourself?

List any unkind thoughts you have towards yourself

Now challenge each of these unkind thoughts.

List any ways you are comparing yourself or your journey to someone else's.

How can you come to terms with or accept where you are at in your journey? How can you stop making comparisons?

Are there any goals you can set for yourself to support the version of you that you want to be?

What is the first step or milestone that would need to be accomplished for each goal you listed? List steps that are bite size, easy to accomplish and that you can get behind to get the ball rolling.

List any labels or negative perceptions that attribute to your lack of self worth. How can you separate the label or perception from your worthiness?

How can you make yourself and what you value within yourself a priority?

What can you do everyday to cultivate a positive self worth and to promote your happiness?

List 20 things you are worthy of or wish to feel worthy of :

-
-
-
-
-
-
-
-
-
-
-
-
-
-
-
-
-
-
-
-

For each thing you listed above, complete the following sentence and answer the question: What would I do, feel and be thinking if I knew without a doubt that I was worthy of _____?

How can you incorporate the answers to the previous question into your daily life? What boundaries would support this? What actions, etc.?

How can you become the version of you who knows and believes they are inherently worthy? What can you do to support yourself and this belief?

What would the version of you that knows and believes in their inherent worthiness not put up with, not allow to happen or not want as part of their life?

SELF ACCEPTANCE AND SELF LOVE

Start this section by listing out all the things you feel are weaknesses, that need improvement, that you do not like or love about yourself.

Remember when I said the universe did not fuck up when it created you? Would you believe me if I told you that all your perceived flaws, weaknesses and things you don't like or love about yourself were created with intention? You may not realize it yet, but much of these qualities you perceive negatively about yourself are actually superpowers, strengths and assets. You just haven't recognized them as such or learned how to utilize them with skill, precision, or positivity.

Often, what we perceive as weaknesses are actually unique perspectives or gifts given to us to help us achieve our purpose in life. Our strengths and perceived weaknesses are tools. Like any other tool, they are neutral. They are neither inherently positive or negative. They can be either a blessing or a curse depending on how we choose to wield them.

Take loyalty, for example—it can be a tremendous asset for maintaining consistency in your life, yet it can become a hindrance when it prevents you from letting go of negative situations. Similarly, extreme sensitivity might make you susceptible to negative feedback, but it can also provide you with a unique perspective on compassion for others. The crucial point here is how you choose to use the tools in your toolbox matter. The intentions you set for them matter.

What many fail to realize is that your strengths are only strengths because of the experience, effort and skill behind them. Just like a muscle, you've developed and honed these particular skills over time causing this tool to be used with more ease. Interestingly, these strengths not only serve their specific purposes but can also help build and cultivate other strengths. They frequently complement and support your perceived weaknesses, enabling you to utilize them more effectively.

Through embracing unconditional love and acceptance for yourself and all the tools in your toolbox, free from judgment, you cultivate the ability to empower yourself. This mindset not only facilitates the further development of your strengths but also empowers you to reshape your perceived weaknesses into strengths.

How could the list you gave in the previous question be harnessed to work in your favor? How can that list be turned into or perceived as a strength or asset? What unique perspectives or opportunities could it provide?

List your strengths, the things you love about yourself and why you feel love or confidence in these areas.

In what ways do or can your strengths compliment or support your percieved weaknesses?

How can your strengths and perceived weaknesses provide opportunities in your life and in your work? How can they make a difference in your life and the lives of others? In what ways do they help you stand out?

LEARNING TO ACCEPT AND LOVE YOURSELF

The reason I had you begin with your perceived weaknesses is because it's often effortless to fixate on the aspects of ourselves we dislike or where we believe we fall short. My intention with this exercise is to offer you a fresh, positive perspective on what you've been regarding as negatives and to equip you with a new tool to help you focus on and nurture positive energy. When you are feeling low focus on your strengths and how your perceived weaknesses are hidden assets.

Here's the crux of truly loving and accepting yourself: it requires unconditional acceptance and love for every facet of your authentic self, both the beautiful and the dark, twisty parts you may perceive as imperfections. What makes love and acceptance so profound is that perfection isn't a requirement.

We've all experienced or known someone who clings to a seemingly insignificant item for years. Whether it's a pair of lucky socks missing a toe, a chipped teacup, an old photograph or a broken locket passed down from a loved one, the item might be aged, imperfect, of little monetary value, or even broken. Yet, we cherish it because it holds a unique significance and value to us.

Much like a priceless piece of art showcased in a museum, you are truly one of a kind. There is no one in the entire universe who possesses the exact same thoughts, perspectives, and uniqueness as you. Learn to recognize this value and treat it as the priceless treasure that it truly is. Even more importantly, learn to grant yourself the same love and acceptance during the good times, but especially during the bad times.

RECOGNIZING & SUPPORTING THE AUTHENTIC SELF

As you become more self-aware, you'll naturally cultivate deeper acceptance, love, confidence, trust and self-esteem. Only you hold the ability to truly recognize your authentic self and determine what nurtures that essence. You decide who you are, who you want to be and how you evolve. Sometimes, our pain, fears, insecurities, or distractions can veer us away from this authentic path. Part of loving and accepting yourself involves acknowledging when change or improvement is necessary to support that authenticity, and approaching it with a compassionate intention. Throughout this journey of improvement, it's crucial to maintain self-love and acceptance through any and all cycles of transformation.

This process includes understanding the motivations driving our desires for self-improvement and ensuring they resonate with our authenticity. Seeking change to align with your genuine aspirations or to amplify your true essence differs significantly from doing so to conform to external expectations or due to feelings of unworthiness. If improvement is warranted, ensure that your desire for change is fueled by a positive and aligned intention that empowers your authentic self.

To the best of your abilities, write down any details you can think of that describe your authentic self and what amplifies your authentic self.

List anything you feel is currently not in alignment with your authentic self, what you can do to make improvements and how can these improvements empower your authentic self moving forward.

How can you better accept yourself for who you really are? How can you support your authentic self?

How can you better love yourself for who you really are? How can you show this love to yourself on a daily basis? Where can you give more compassion?

What would the version of you who fully accepts and loves themself be doing, thinking and feeling?

CHAPTER *Thirteen*

CLOSING

Congratulations! You've reached the final chapter of this journal. Before we go any further, I want to express how proud I am of you. Your dedication and openness to exploring new perspectives on yourself and the world around you are truly commendable. Take a moment to acknowledge your own achievements, recognize the progress you've made, and feel proud of yourself. Allow yourself to take a deep breath, exhale a big sigh, and bask in your accomplishments. Although your journey does not end here, this is a moment for you to celebrate all the strides you've taken towards personal growth and self-discovery.

At the outset of this journal, I had you take this evaluation to provide a snapshot of your starting point. Now, we'll revisit it to offer you a tangible representation of the progress you've achieved and the distance you've traveled since then.

HOW DO YOU FEEL PHYSICALLY RIGHT NOW?

HOW DO YOU FEEL MENTALLY RIGHT NOW?

HOW DO YOU FEEL EMOTIONALLY RIGHT NOW?

HOW DO YOU FEEL SPIRITUALLY RIGHT NOW?

WHAT IS CONTRIBUTING TO HOW YOU FEEL PHYSICALLY?

WHAT IS CONTRIBUTING TO HOW YOU FEEL MENTALLY?

WHAT IS CONTRIBUTING TO HOW YOU FEEL EMOTIONALLY?

WHAT IS CONTRIBUTING TO HOW YOU FEEL SPIRITUALLY?

Rate Your Self Confidence

1 2 3 4 5 ___

No Confidence — Feeling Confident

Why did you give yourself this score?

What things contribute to your self confidence?

What things contribute to your lack of self confidence?

Rate Your Self Worth

1 2 3 4 5 ___

Not worthy — I Know My Worth

Why did you give yourself this score?

What things contribute to your self worth?

What things contribute to your lack of self worth?

Rate Your Value

1 2 3 4 5 ___

I Don't Feel Valuable — I Know My Value

Why did you give yourself this score?

What things contribute to your value?

What things contribute to feeling like you are less valuable?

HOW DO YOU KNOW WHEN "THE WORK" IS DONE?

I often receive this question, and truthfully, it's one I used to ponder myself. How do you determine when the inner work, or "the work" in general, is complete? How do you recognize the shift from transitioning to embodying what you desire? How do you know when you're truly prepared for what lies ahead?

As I stated at the beginning of this book, and I reiterate now: there's no distinct line between where you are and where you want to be. Your journey is uniquely yours and it is not alway linear. While the understanding that things are as they are may come suddenly, there won't necessarily be a clear moment where you can identify crossing the finish line. Your journey will continuously evolve, much like you do. However, what I can tell you is that the work concludes as you finish it. It's typically a gradual process and transition.

As you engage in the work, you'll begin to sense a feeling of completion, acceptance, or peace. The urge or longing to revisit the past or return to old ways will diminish. Your optimism towards the future will outweigh your regrets or disappointments of the past. Your pain will no longer overshadow your joy. You will reach a point where you decide and affirm that the work is finished. You will have provided yourself with all the necessary support. Your thoughts, feelings, and being will undergo a transformation. The changes you've implemented will no longer feel like conscious efforts but will become second nature and automatic.

Ultimately, the work concludes when you decide it is. When you feel there's nothing further to say or do. The work is complete when you know it is complete.

THE JOURNEY DOESN'T END HERE

Although this chapter is coming to an end, your journey doesn't end at the close of this book. My hope is that this journal has assisted you along your path of self discovery and healing. Whether you feel there is still work to be done in this particular era of your journey or you feel you are ready for whatever comes next, know that you owe it to yourself to continue to nurture unconditional self love and be your own soulmate. Above all, remember that you owe it to yourself to never give up on you and the you that you want to be.

Thank-you!

To All My Valued Readers,

I want to take a moment to express my sincere gratitude to all of you. Each of your journeys is uniquely personal, and I feel deeply honored to have the opportunity to be a part of them. What you may not realize is that by joining this community, you're contributing to a larger purpose. Your decision to purchase this book and your support through reviews and word of mouth are invaluable in helping me make a greater positive impact. Your involvement extends beyond personal growth—it's part of a collective effort to effect positive change, getting this journal in the hands of more people who need it. Thank you for being a vital part of this shared mission and for your ongoing support. Publishing this journal has been a dream come true and you have been instrumental in the manifestation of that dream.

I wish you continued joy as you continue on your journey. And as always, may your life be full of light, full of love, gratitude and abundance.

Until We Meet Again,

Blake Holloway

About
BLAKE C. HOLLAWAY

Blake C. Hollaway is a spiritual thought leader and transformation and manifestation coach. Her journey into spiritual coaching was inspired by her own journey of surviving abuse and undergoing self-recovery and transformation. Having struggled with breaking generational karmic cycles, low self-worth, and deeply ingrained learned behavior, she intimately understands the emotional and physical toll that a loss of self can take. Her personal triumph over these challenges became the catalyst for her mission to empower others and teach them self love. Through the integration of spiritual practices and practical advice, her teachings have positively impacted individuals worldwide. Find Blake at www.blakechollaway.com or on social media @blakechollaway.

ACKNOWLEDGEMENTS

Thank you to my mom, without whom this book would not have been possible. Your unwavering support has been a constant source of encouragement throughout the years, especially during the process of writing and publishing this book. Thank you for being there during my most challenging moments and not allowing me to give up on myself when my life was at its darkest. You taught me how to define life on my own terms and how to fight impossible battles. Your support in all these moments has provided me with the resilience and strength that ultimately paved the way for the creation of these pages and will now light a path for so many others through the darkness.

www.ingramcontent.com/pod-product-compliance
Lightning Source LLC
Chambersburg PA
CBHW080836120626
46553CB00009B/2458

* 9 7 9 8 9 9 0 3 8 4 0 0 2 *